Children Figurines
of Bisque and Chinawares
1850-1950

Elyse Zorn Karlin

D1494130

1469 Morstein Road, West Chester, Pennsylvania 19380

Dedication

This book is dedicated to my favorite child, my son, Harris, and to my husband, Andrew, for patience while I was writing.

05268885

Published by Schiffer Publishing, Ltd.
1469 Morstein Road
West Chester, Pennsylvania 19380
Please write for a free catalog.
This book may be purchased from the publisher.
Please include $2.00 postage.
Try your bookstore first.

Printed in the United States of America.
ISBN: 0-88740-297-6

We are interested in hearing from authors with book ideas on related topics.

Contents

A boy and girl piano baby, both of German origin. *Author's collection. Photo by Laurie Morrison.*

Acknowledgments

I gratefully acknowledge help in writing this book from the following people:

Sanie Acowitz; Christopher Bensch, Strong Museum, Rochester, New York; Bunny Campione, Sotheby's Auction House, London; Marvin Cohen, Marvin Cohen Auctions, New Lebanon, New Hampshire; Lillian Cohen; Liz Donnelly; Mildred Ewing, Skinner's Auction House, Bolton, Massachusetts; Kathy Fable; Diane Freer; Joe and Dorothy Haber; Sarah Hamill, Skinner's Auction House; Jerry Hart, Jerry Hart Galleries, Houston, Texas; Penny Hadfield; Daniel Jacoby; Jim Julia, James D. Julia, Inc., Fairfield, Maine; Jenny Jones; Shirley Lipnick; Connie Lee Martin; Laurie Morrison; Linda Phipps, Theriault's Auctions, Annapolis, Maryland; Joyce Pimentel; Linda Rehak; Nancy Schiffer, my editor; Randy Selnick; Karen Stewart, President, International Rose O'Neill Club, Branson, Missouri; Andrew Swanson; George and Florence Theriault; Countess Maria Von Staufer, Christmas Archives, Cardiff, Wales; Rose Marie Willruth; and Carolyn Zorn, my sister.

4-piece jazz group of young black musicians, 2⅛" high. *Author's collection.*

Preface

Almost twenty years ago, when I was setting up a home of my own, my aunt, who was an avid antiques collector, opened up her china cabinet and handed me two figurines of babies lying on their backs kicking their feet in the air. I was charmed by them, but didn't really know what they were. As I began to attend flea markets and antique shows myself, I learned that they were "piano babies." Soon I was "hooked"—and I began to collect a variety of children figurines.

Through the years I've found it difficult to obtain information about the various types of figurines I was purchasing. Most of what I learned was told to me by dealers—some more knowledgeable than others. Eventually I found information on some of the figurines sandwiched in small spaces in books on dolls, but I wasn't very satisfied. I felt that figurine collectors needed their own reference.

When I finally set out to provide the book I wanted myself, I had a problem determining how to define which types of figurines to include. The following is the criteria I finally developed:

1. *They are made of bisque or china (porcelain)*. Figurines of chalkware, metal, celluloid, composition, and other materials are not included in this book. However, wherever relevant, I will mention that these other figurines do exist.

2. *They have no moveable parts*. Essentially I feel that a figurine that has arms and legs that move, or it bends at the waist, falls into the doll category. However, I have made a few exceptions. If a figurine was made also in a doll version, both will be discussed. Also, I do include nodders, which I consider as figurines because their bodies do not move or bend in any way although their heads move.

3. *They were not meant to be dressed*. These figurines either have molded clothing or were meant to have none, unlike dolls that were mostly made to be clothed. Sometimes children (and adults) dress some of these figurines, such as Frozen Charlottes. Examples of dressed figurines are included.

School boy and girl in winter coats. Each with unusual spectacles. 7˝ high. The girl's eyeglasses no longer stay in place. *Author's collection.*

Kewpie fairy with candy holder.
Collection of Rose Marie Willruth.
Photo by Laurie Morrison.

4. *They have molded hair or painted-on hair.* A few examples of Frozen Charlottes and piano babies have wigs, but for the most part figurines were made with representations of hair.

5. *They are no longer being manufactured from original molds.* However, reproductions of some of them still are being made.

6. The figurines in this book were *almost all made in Germany* except for the Japanese copies, which are also illustrated. Some porcelain figurines were made in England, France, and the United States, but by-and-large the collectible pieces today are German in origin.

7. *These figurines were produced primarily as novelty items, not as playthings.* Although decorative, some were used as toys (such as Frozen Charlottes), but they were not very flexible as toys.

8. *I have excluded a few manufacturers of figurines that made very few examples of children figurines,* such as Meissen, Royal Dux, Staffordshire, and Sevres. Hummel figurines are not covered here since they are still being made today.

Please bear in mind when using this book that there is now much less documentation about figurines than there is about dolls and many other types of collectibles. I've presented the best information I could find, even when it is at times somewhat conflicting. I will be more than happy to hear from everyone who has additional information.

New Rochelle, New York
August 1990.

Chapter 1

Bisque and China Children Figurines

Between the years 1850 and 1950 a great many types of children figurines were manufactured, most in Germany. Those that are included in this study were not made with the intent that they would be collectibles, as are many figurines being made today; these figurines were merely created to be decorations in the home. Many of these were used popularly until the 1930s when, in general, their appeal had diminished.

Many of the baby and children figurines fall into specific categories with specific names as reflected in the chapters here. Many fall into a "general" category that includes figurines of many shapes, sizes, and descriptions. Literally hundreds of porcelain factories in Germany made them, and numerous types and levels of quality exist. While some also were made in France, England, and the United States, or were copied from German originals in Japan, most are from Germany and have been exported to England and the United States.

Left, Young boy making a muscle, with Limbach mark, similar to Heubach action figurines, "Made in Germany," 4″ high. Right, Young boy kicking soccer ball, 5¼″ high.

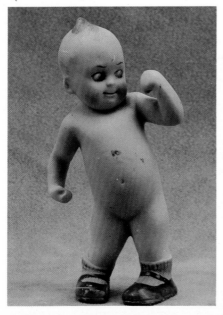

Little girl with blue gown holding kittens in her dress. Red and white dog on side and grey and white cat under her feet. Bisque, 6" high. *Courtesy of James D. Julia, Inc.*

Nice large bisque figurine of a school girl. Detail all around. 13" high, marked "R" in blue stamp in diamond shape, "43" incised, "R6184" incised, "38" painted on bottom. *Author's collection. Photo by Diane Freer.*

The "general" category will be the first to be explored.

The figurines were of every kind imaginable; bisque or china or a combination of both, very simple to very elaborate, tiny (one inch) to as tall as a foot or more. They range from the highly decorated to the very plain.

The bulk of these figurines do not carry a manufacturer's mark. When they do, and if it is traceable, the figurine's value is increased. A great many have a number incised or painted on them that is either a style, model, inventory, or mold number. As far as has been determined, these numbers alone (unlike some numbers on dolls) can't be traced to a particular manufacturer without the company name or mark accompanying it. The presence of these numbers tends to indicate German origin. The

Bisque child road sweeper. English, 1880s. *Courtesy Christmas Archives (U.K.) Ltd.*

word "Germany" stamped on the bottom or "Made in Germany" is also desirable. However, even if German, the quality of figurines can vary greatly as there were so many different manufacturers.

Later Japanese versions of these figurines sometimes can be charming and desirable, but in general they do not command the same prices. Some are marked "Made in Japan," while others have even, perfectly matched-in-size numbers stamped on them.

The best way to differentiate between German figurines and Japanese versions is to look at as many as possible. You will begin to recognize the differences with the more examples of each you see. German bisque is clearly of higher quality and the molding was usually far more detailed. Japanese bisque is more yellow rather than "rosy" like the German bisque.

Some of the German manufacturers include:

Alt, Beck, Gottschalck
Koch & Fisher Dornheim
Johann Christian Eberlein
F.W. Goebel
Hertwig & Co.
Julius Heubach
A.W. Fr. Kister
Kley and Hahn

August Riedler
Royal Rudolstadt
Simon and Halbig
Theodor Pohl
Gebruder Heubach
Limbach
Kling & Co.

Bisque girl in real lace dress that has been glazed and hardened. *Author's collection. Photo by Diane Freer.*

Reverse of girl in lace dress. Note how the detail continues around the back. She has two metal prongs in her base...perhaps she was a cake decoration.

Conta and Boehm and Ernest Bohne were some of the most prolific.

When purchasing any type of figurine, look for the following points to get the best value:

—Avoid cracks, chips, repairs. Look for good general condition.

—Decoration (paint) should still be intact.

—Choose one signed by the manufacturer and/or with a number or "Germany" marked on it.

—Avoid a reproduction.

—An unusual pose, subject matter, or detail is preferable.

—Very small or very large size is more interesting.

Don't be surprised if a figurine engaged in a sports activity— tennis or golf—commands a higher price. They are also in a category of sports collectibles.

Black figurines may sell for higher prices because they are harder to find and are also collected as part of black memorabilia. Black models are usually the most rare to find in any figurine category. They tend to be stereotypical—a boy eating a watermelon—and at times can be derogatory in nature, which unfortunately is a reflection of the time in which they were made.

A word of warning: Reproduction figurines are being sold today to the antique trade. While they may be sold to a dealer as a "repro," the dealer will not necessarily pass along this fact. Some of the more common "repro" figurines include:

—Bisque boy with rabbit and girl with dove pair, 13 inches high.

—Bisque boy and girl pair with broken toys. Both wear hats and shoes with ankle straps; 16 inches high.

—Bisque boy with fruit and girl with flowers pair. Both wearing nineteenth-century clothing. Approximately nine inches high.

It is not known if they have any markings.

Marks: The following are some marks to look for. They are not necessarily easy to find.

This is not to say that you should pass up a wonderful unsigned piece, but signed pieces have higher resale value.

AUGUST RIEDLER

HEUBACH
SUNBURST
MARK

KLING & CO.

LIMBACH

OTHER
HEUBACH
MARKS

F. & W. GOEBEL

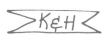

KLEY & HAHN

HEUBACH
SQUARE
MARK

(Stamped in blue)

ROYAL RUDOLSTADT

CONTA & BOEHM

ERNST
BOHNE

Boy sitting in egg. Has Heubach-like quality but Goebel mark on the bottom. Bisque, 6" high. *Author's collection. Photo by Laurie Morrison.*

Base of boy in egg showing Goebel mark.

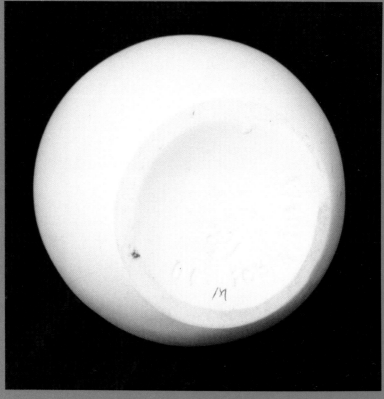

Bisque boy with school book. Nice detail; 9" high. *Author's collection.* *Photo by Laurie Morrison.*

Back of bisque boy figurine. Detail continues around back with book bag over boy's shoulder. Incised "5111" at base. *Photo by Laurie Morrison.*

Pair of children figurines, china with bisque bases, circa 1920. Interesting "nubby" look on sweaters (raised bumps) and gold trim. Incised "Made in Germany" under glaze. Facial features painted a little lopsided, 5½" high. *Author's collection. Photo by Laurie Morrison.*

Young bisque girl with basket of fruit. Molding not high quality but nice decoration with gold trim. There are uniform small holes in basket, might have been to hold "posies." Probably German, circa 1930, 6¾" high. *Author's collection, Photo by Diane Freer.*

Small figurine doing "morning stretch." Bisque with numbers incised on bottom but not readable; 2¾" high. *Author's collection. Photo by Laurie Morrison.*

Superb Victorian bisque baby in straw trunk. Applied multicolored floral decoration. Baby has a soft pink-and-white gown and blue-and-white striped sock. Reads "cabin baggage" on front of piece. Either German or French. "Déposé" mark on bottom; 7½" high by 6" on the side. *Photo courtesy James D. Julia, Inc.*

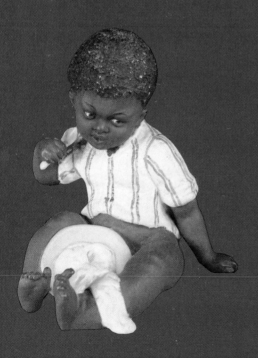

Black boy in bisque with spilled porridge. Documented as Heubach, but has no marks; 5½" high. Stamped "Made in Germany" in circle in red ink. *Author's collection. Photo by Laurie Morrison.*

Dutch girl figurine with same "nubby" look on dress and gold trim. Also china and bisque; 6" high. *Author's collection. Photo by Diane Freer.*

Back of Dutch girl. Molding work goes all the way around but not the painting. Marked "Made in Germany" on back, incised "250" on base.

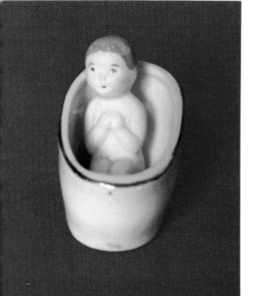

This small bisque boy looks like he's freezing. He is sitting in a china bathtub. This piece may have been imported by B. Shackman & Co., which imported pieces like this. Boy is 1⅝" high, tub is 2½" long. *Author's collection. Photo by Diane Freer.*

Beautiful pair of bisque babies in
carriages. 8½" high. *Photo courtesy of
James D. Julia, Inc.*

A number of German bisque figurines
were made to be hung from a shelf by a
wire or thin ribbon. This little girl is
sitting on a horn. 3¼" high by 4" long,
no marks. *Author's collection. Photo by
Diane Freer.*

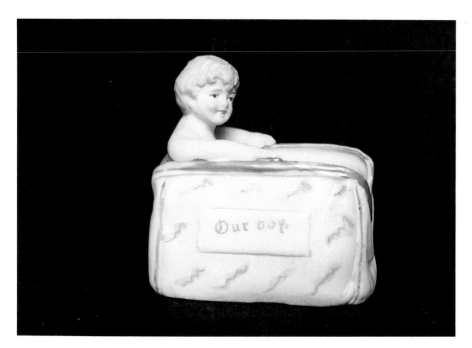

Little boy sitting in a suitcase. Reads "our boy" on front. He is wearing white pajama bottom drawstring pants with nice detail. Gold trim on the suitcase. Stamped "Made in Germany." 4" high. *Author's collection. Photo by Laurie Morrison.*

Rub-a-dub-dub. These two nude bisque boys look remarkably similar and may have been made by the same manufacturer. (The tub is not old.) Front figure is 2¾" high with no marks. The boy in the back is 3" high and has some indecipherable numbers in the back. *Author's collection. Photo by Diane Freer.*

Black bisque girl on chamber pot with an umbrella. She is marked "L" on her foot in red and is 4¾" high. The brown girl also sitting on a chamber pot holds a green and yellow melon. 5" high, and is marked "4418" and "Germany." *Collection of Jenny Jones. Photo by Jim Yarbrough.*

This little black bisque boy looks like he's bundled up to be delivered by the stork. There is a small hole at the top of the figurine for it to be hung. The Strong Museum has a similar piece to this one but it has not only the black baby's head but also a white baby's head on the side where the black baby's feet are sticking out. German, no marks. 4" high. *Author's collection. Photo by Diane Freer.*

"The potty" (chamber pot) was a favorite subject in child figurines. This bisque pair of a white and black baby are kissing while they are on the potty. 3¼" high. *Strong Museum, Rochester, New York.*

A child holding a chamber pot. Bisque, 5" high. *Strong Museum, Rochester, New York.*

A group of china angels engaged in various activities imported from Germany by B. Shackman & Co., New York City. *Collection of Daniel Jacoby. Photo by Laurie Morrison.*

Two charming 7½" high bisque figurine pairs holding umbrellas. *Photos courtesy of James D. Julia, Inc.*

Cherubs and angels were another popular Victorian figurine. Small bisque angel with gold trim. 1⅞" high. *Author's collection. Photo by Diane Freer.*

Chapter 2
Piano Babies

Piano baby figurines were made in many different and charming poses to capture the essence of babyhood. Until about the 1870s crawling was not really acceptable to Victorian parents (children were encouraged to walk as soon as possible). Piano babies represented one of the first depictions of children crawling in a "mass market" item. They are all-bisque with molded hair and clothes, painted, and range in size from a few inches to 20 inches.

Piano babies were Victorian knick-knacks used to hold the ever-present shawl in place on a family's piano. They were made primarily in Germany beginning in the 1880s and continued to be made until the 1930s, although the quality declined by then. In the 1930s they were copied in Japan, and reproductions have continued to be made even up to the present.

The most valuable piano babies are those manufactured by Gebruder Heubach, being prized by both American and British collectors. The Heubach company often used the same head for its piano babies as for it's dolls' heads. It is not unusual to find several versions or sizes of the same piano baby, a fact particularly well documented with Heubach piano babies.

Parian-type piano baby holding up gown. 2½" high. *Author's collection. Photo by Laurie Morrison.*

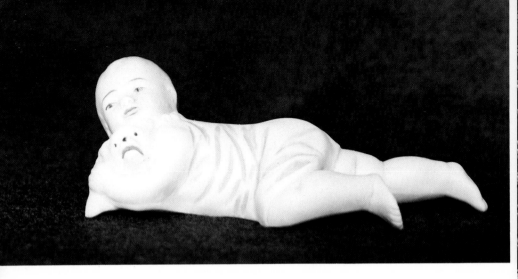

Piano baby with dog. No marks.
German. 6¼" high. *Author's collection.*
Photo by Diane Freer.

Piano babies were made in three types of bisque: tinted bisque, a parian-like bisque, and brown bisque. The tinted bisque figurines (the majority) have a rosy color to the skin. The parian-type are very white with no color added. The brown versions have had the bisque painted after it was fired. The parian-type seem to be the oldest piano babies, as they are the plainest. As Victorian taste became more fussy in the latter part of the period, so, too, did figurines become more highly decorated.

More unusual pieces include:

a baby in a chair, with a bonnet
in a shoe or other object
with glued-on hair (mohair wig)
with gold beading on clothing
with intaglio eyes (a feature of Heubach piano babies).

Condition is very important. The original paint and bisque should be intact. Make certain no repairs have been made. It's a good idea to run your fingers over the feet and fingers of piano babies, as these are the places likely to chip and this often goes unnoticed when you first look at a figurine.

Reproductions are generally of a lesser quality and quite easy to spot. Some may be stamped "Made in Japan" or still have an Oriental manufacturer's label on the bottom. The inferior quality and detail of Oriental reproductions is easy to see when compared with an earlier German piano baby. The eyes may look somewhat Oriental and the skin tone of the bisque is more sallow. The quality of the bisque is usually inferior as well.

There are modern piano babies currently being wholesaled to antiques dealers. They include a pair featuring a boy and a girl

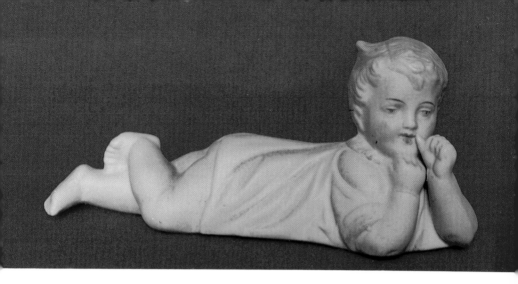

Piano baby sucking his thumb. German.
No marks. 5½" long. *Author's collection.*
Photo by Diane Freer.

wearing wide brimmed hats. They are both barefoot and are 13 inches high. The girl appears to be like one made by a giftware manufacturer labeled "Andrea." An antiques dealer has reported that "Andrea" has been making piano babies since the 1950s.

Marks:
Many piano babies are unsigned. Some are marked "Germany" or "Made in Germany" while others have some numbers incised in the bottom. If you are fortunate enough to find a signed piece, the following are some of the marks you may find:

Heubach—had many different marks but these are the ones that are commonly found on piano babies. In addition to the Heubach mark, a piece may have a set of numbers stamped or incised on it, "Made in Germany" stamped or incised on it, and the word "déposé" or "dep" (as previously noted) which means it is a registered trademark.

Heubach Marks

Royal Rudolstadt—RW stamped in blue, may have "Germany" and an incised number.

RW

Royal Rudolstadt

Limbach

Conta & Boehm

Kling & Co.

Dressel & Kister

DEP

Karl Schneider

J.D. Kestner

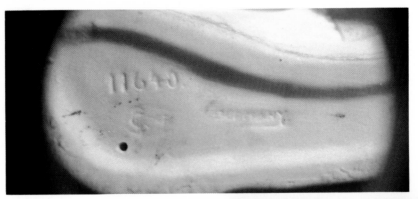

Ernst Bohne

Very simple girl piano baby with short hair. Her bib says "Papa's Darling." A very similar piece in the Strong Museum reads "Momma's Pet" on the bib. "3987" on the back. 4¾" high. *Author's collection. Photo by Diane Freer.*

Two very similar piano babies with dogs. Note the differences in quality. They probably were made by two different manufacturers and the one on the right may be Japanese. The rattle in the mouth of the piano baby to the left is glazed, and there is gold beading on his night shirt...clearly a better-made piece. The figurine to the left is 6¼" long by 2¾" high. The smaller figurine is 5⅛" long by 2⅜" high. *Author's collection. Photo by Diane Freer.*

A different look at a piano baby with a dog. Very nice detail on clothing. No marks; 9" long, 5¼" high. *Collection of Shirley Lipnick. Photo by Laurie Morrison.*

Piano babies often hold objects in their hands. This 6" high girl with very nice clothing holds a piece of fruit. She has gold beading on her dress. The sweet 5" high boy with one sock holds a rattle. No marks. *Author's collection. Photo by Laurie Morrison.*

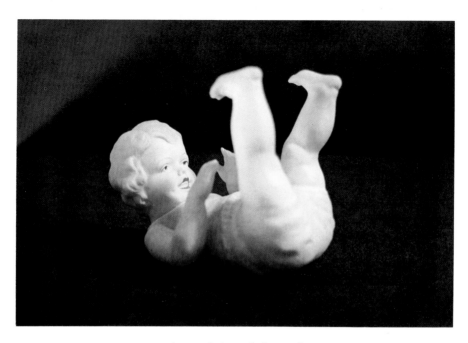

Typical piano baby with feet in the air and playing with his hands. 4" high by 5" long. *Author's collection. Photo by Laurie Morrison.*

Medium-quality girl piano baby. White on white decoration on nightgown, with only one sock. 4¾" high, 5¾" long. Incised "06 88 and 85" on bottom, "57" painted on. *Author's collection. Photo by Diane Freer.*

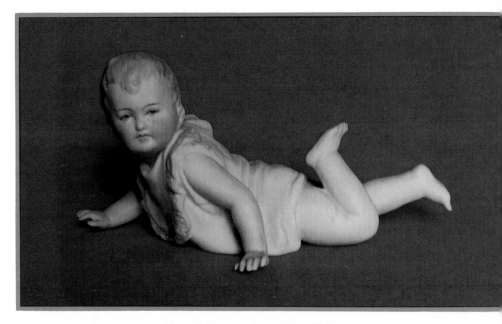

Piano baby wearing a bib. 8" long.
Incised "646" on bottom. German.
*Author's collection. Photo by Diane
Freer.*

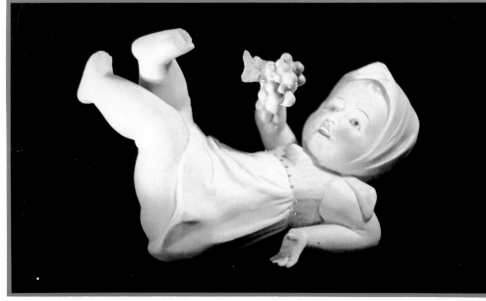

Large piano baby eating grapes. She has
intaglio eyes and gold beading on her
dress. 10" long by 6" high. Incised
"Germany," "11640," and appears to
have a manufacturer's mark that is not
readable. *Author's collection. Photo by
Laurie Morrison.*

Large bisque piano baby with thumb in mouth. Nice details on clothing including gold beading. No marks. 11" high. *Collection of Shirley Lipnick.* *Photo by Laurie Morrison.*

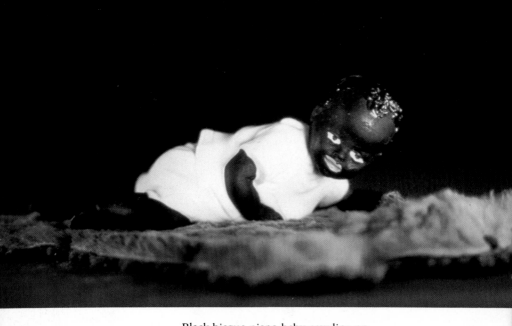

Black bisque piano baby crawling on bearskin rug. Intaglio eyes. German, no maker's marks but marked "350" on bottom. 4½" long, 1½" high. *Collection of Jenny Jones. Photo by Jim Yarbrough.*

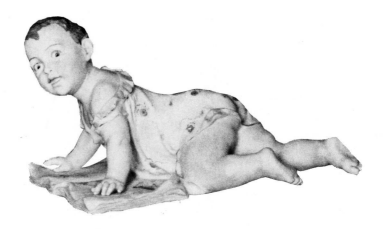

Large seated piano baby girl with bow on dress. No marks, but label on bottom reads "July 30, 1907...Happy Birthday Grandma." 8½" high. *Collection of Shirley Lipnick. Photo by Laurie Morrison.*

Another similar large piano baby girl with beading on dress. "1119" stamped on bottom. 11" high. *Collection of Shirley Lipnick. Photo by Laurie Morrison.*

Opposite page:
Outstanding large piano baby crawling on his hands and knees with his hands on a book. Very fine decoration with floral pattern and gold beading on gown. Book has painted words "duck" and "donkey" on pages. Incised "5540" on base. 16" long. *Photo courtesy of James D. Julia, Inc.*

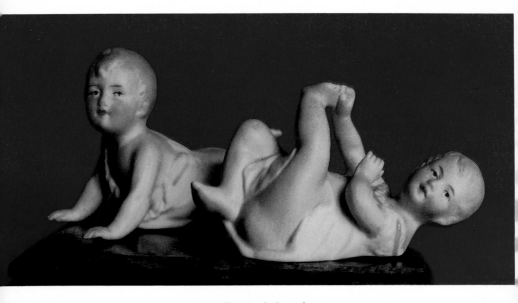

Two small piano babies that appear to be the same baby in different poses. Not signed but possibly by Heubach. 4" long, 3½" high. *Author's collection. Photo by Diane Freer.*

Piano baby with two Siamese kittens. Very colorful floral decoration on yellow dress. Probably French. 9" long. *Photo courtesy of James D. Julia, Inc.*

Charming plump piano baby in walker. Looks similar to many Heubach pieces. 7" high. Incised "8816." *Author's collection. Photo by Laurie Morrison.*

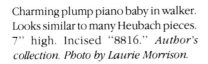

The piano baby on the right is 8½" long and wears a light blue gown with delicate lavender flowers. The baby has a rabbit under its arm and a Siamese cat on its back. Possibly French. The piano baby on the left has pink rose decoration on her blue trimmed yellow dress. 10" long, 5" high. *Photo courtesy of James D. Julia, Inc.*

Pair of piano babies that are most likely Japanese. The quality of the bisque is not very good and the molding is not at all delicate. "73/112" and "73/113" painted on bottoms. *Author's collection. Photo by Diane Freer.*

Piano baby girl with original mohair wig. 4¼" high. *Strong Museum, Rochester, New York.*

Parian-type piano baby holding fruit. 5" high. Marked "Germany KH 58" on back. *Collection of Connie Lee Martin.*

Pair of Japanese piano babies holding animals. The bisque is not of the quality of German bisque and has a yellowish tint to it. The remnants of a paper label are still on one of the figurines. 5½" high by 7¾" long. *Author's collection. Photo by Laurie Morrison.*

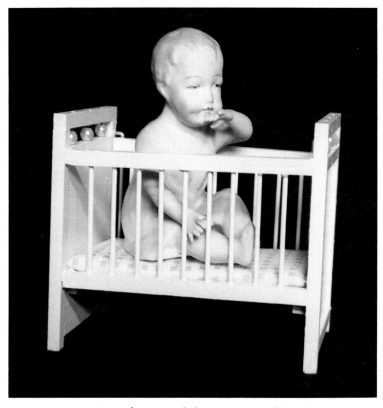

Very plain piano baby sitting in a crib. May be Japanese. Painted "IU" on bottom. 3¾" *Author's collection. Photo by Diane Freer.*

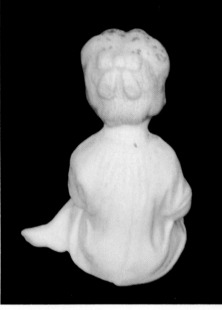

Parian-type piano baby girl with shoes in her hand. Very plain, but very sweet. No marks, 2 " high. *Author's collection. Photo by Diane Freer.*

Detail of parian girl's head. Hair is molded with great detail, including bow.

Piano baby with red and white dog in arms. Floral pattern on blue gown with gilt beading. 8" high. *Photo courtesy of James D. Julia, Inc.*

Chapter 3

Gebruder Heubach: 1820-1945

Gebruder Heubach (Heubach Brothers) is widely recognized as being the premiere German manufacturer of bisque figurines as well as an important manufacturer of doll's heads. The company was originally founded in 1820 in Thuringia, (East) Germany, and continued in business after 1945 in Goslar, (West) Germany although no longer making figurines and dolls. Unfortunately, most of their company archives were left behind when they fled East Germany in 1945.

Heubach specialized in bisque which is well-suited to producing lifelike coloring in figurines and dolls. They are famous for their bisque figures, which they continued to produce until the 1920s. They were years ahead of other manufacturers in achieving a look of a "real child."

In addition to the realistic faces of Heubach figurines, a noticeable characteristic is their attention to detail. Dresses are painstakingly decorated with small designs or gold beading, and the style of clothing is true to its time period. Designs continued around the entire figurine, and deep sculpture in the molding adds to its beauty.

Their figurines are also known for their intaglio eyes, which add to the realistic appearance. While most figurines' eyes are painted on "flat," intaglio eyes are painted on eyeballs that are rounded in the molding process. The pupil and iris are incised for depth, the pupil is painted larger than the iris and a raised white dot creates a highlight. Eyelashes sometimes are painted on. One additional point—the figurines almost always had blonde hair.

Heubach made a wide variety of baby and child figurines including piano babies, and probably the small snow babies. They are known to have made the "Cliquot Club" Snow baby (see snow baby chapter for illustration). In addition, children's figurines in the following categories are well-documented:

1. *Dutch boys and girls.* These figurines are found alone and in pairs, sometimes carrying baskets on their back with Easter eggs, milk buckets, and so forth. They are either orange with green or blue and were made in several sizes.

A favorite theme....bathing children. The seated boy with the delightful bathing cap has an incised sunburst mark. He is approximately 6" high. *Collection of Shirley Lipnick. Photo by Laurie Morrison.*

2. *Children with Easter Eggs and Easter Bunny Children.* The eggs are open and were probably filled with Easter candy. Some of the eggs have lids. The Easter Bunny Children are dressed in bunny suits. The largest is 14" high.

3. *Position babies and action babies.* Position babies were probably modelled after Rose O'Neill's Kewpies yet these nude figurines have a look of their own. They are in various endearing positions a young baby might be found in—the action or "naughty" babies have angry looks and clenched fists as a small child does when throwing a tantrum. Although unclothed, some have molded boots or shoes. Rare black versions do exist.

4. *Naked babies and babies in bath tubs* were also a common theme in Heubach figurines. They were also made by a number of other German porcelain manufacturers.

5. *Child figurines in a variety of activities.* Many of the beautiful child figurines manufactured by Heubach don't fall into an overall category. Examples include children holding animals, newsboys, children playing "grown-up," children sitting in chairs, dancing girls, Oriental girls and boys in costumes, babies in shoes, children in high chairs, young girls and boys in their "best" clothes, etc. Gebruder Heubach also made beautiful adult and animal figurines.

This small bather sits in a china tub. This was a souvenir piece and reads "From Canada" on the front in gold. Heubach sunburst mark incised on bottom under glaze and "70." "117" painted over glaze. 3" high. *Author's collection. Photo by Laurie Morrison.*

In addition to the huge number of different types of figurines there were numerous variations on the same figurine. Heubach would start with the same design, create it in several sizes, vary the decoration (different colors and detail), add a bonnet etc. Then the same head might be used for a doll as well.

Marks:

Probably more Heubach pieces are found signed than any other manufacturer of this time period, but there are still many unmarked pieces. The best way to tell if an unsigned piece is Heubach is to find a documented piece that is the same or very similar.

Although Gebruder Heubach used a number of marks, the two most commonly found are the sunburst mark and the square mark. The rising sun or sunburst mark was registered in 1882 so any figurines with this mark are after this date. Earlier pieces have the sunburst mark incised (like an intaglio), later ones have it raised (like a cameo). Heubach marks that are stamped are done so in red, blue or green.

For a more comprehensive view of a Heubach collection I suggest you read *Parlor Fancies, the Bisque Figurines of Gebruder Heubach,* which is a wonderfully illustrated catalog of the Louise Carter collection of Heubach figurines auctioned by and available from Theriault's, Box 151, Annapolis, Maryland 21404.

Gebruder Heubach Marks.

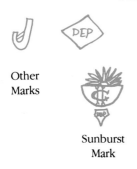

Other
Marks

Sunburst
Mark

Heubach
Square
Mark

Planter with two "position babies," 6" high, square mark incised in bottom. *Collection of Shirley Lipnick. Photo by Laurie Morrison.*

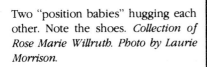

Two "position babies" hugging each other. Note the shoes. *Collection of Rose Marie Willruth. Photo by Laurie Morrison.*

Seated Dutch girl, 3⅜" high. *Author's collection.*

Easter bunny children with eggs are among the most wonderful Heubach creations. Several bear the Heubach square mark and/or a mold number. The eggs probably held candy originally and were used for a variety of uses after Easter. *Courtesy of Theriault's.*

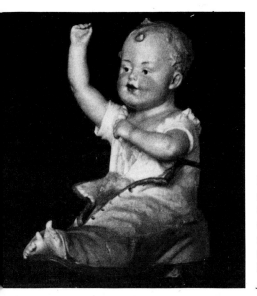

Rare large bisque Heubach piano baby in shoe. Shoe is tattered and child's foot hangs out of one hole. Child is dressed in white gown with blue ribbons. Blonde hair and nicely painted facial features. Shoe is white and light brown. 12" high. *Courtesy of James D. Julia, Inc.*

Opposite page:

A beautiful Victorian girl with a kitten in her muff. This figurine was made in several versions. The detailing is exquisite. She has a sunburst mark and is 15" high. *Courtesy of Theriault's.*

Heubach boy and girl in Sunday dress. Tiny-beaded decoration on clothing is a mark of the Heubach quality. Lovely realistic faces. Sunburst mark, 14" high. *Courtesy of Theriault's.*

A charming pair of Heubach children's busts leaning on logs. 7" high, with the sunburst mark. Girl is also marked "3010" and the boy is marked "3011." *Courtesy of Theriault's.*

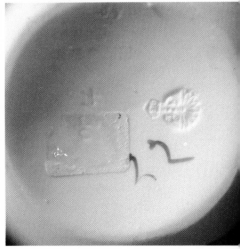

Detail: Heubach square mark on foot of figurine.

Detail: Heubach sunburst mark incised in base of figurine.

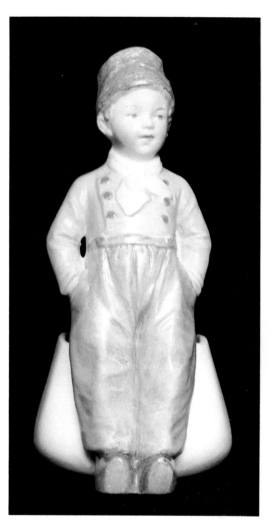

Dutch boy with planter. 6½" high with sunburst mark on base and "4136" and "33" incised. *Author's collection. Photo by Laurie Morrison.*

It is believed that Heubach made snow babies although none are signed. Judging from the quality of these two it is easy to believe they might be Heubach. *Author's collection and collection of Linda Rehak and Andrew Swanson.*

A lovely Heubach dancing girl. This figurine was made in a variety of sizes, this being one of the smallest. The molding detail is excellent although the painting is a bit sloppy. It also was made with several different color dresses. 7½" high. Heubach sunburst mark is "raised" on back and "12685" is incised. *Author's collection. Photo by Diane Freer.*

Back of dancing girl. Notice the detail in the trellis work and the sunburst mark at the base. *Photo by Laurie Morrison.*

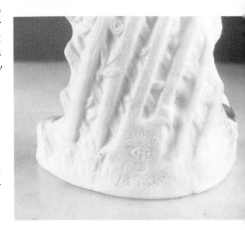

Opposite page:
Two black boys sharing a secret; an example of how well Heubach did black figurines. The features are not exaggerated here as they are on many black figurines of the time. 11" high, sunburst mark. *Courtesy of Theriault's.*

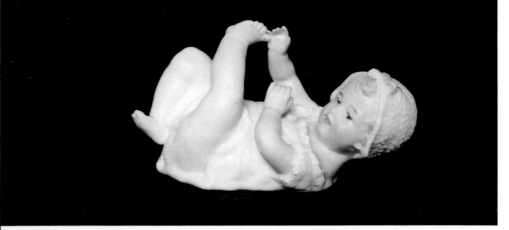

This piano baby playing with his toes was made in several different sizes and is one of the more common Heubach pieces to find. It is known as "Baby Stuart." 4¾" high, sunburst mark "raised" on bottom. *Author's collection, photo by Diane Freer.*

Detail of piano baby's bonnet. Note the care that was taken to make the bonnet look like it was crocheted—a typical Heubach detail.

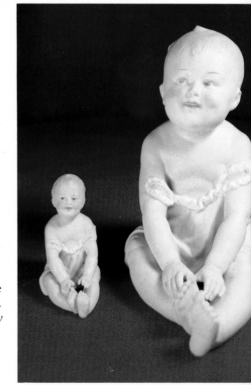

Two piano babies. An example of the same figurine in different sizes. *Collection of Shirley Lipnick. Photo by Laurie Morrison.*

Some enterprising person turned this wonderful and large (13½") Heubach girl with a sea shell into a lamp. She needs some restoration on her elbow. The flowers on her dress are painted in beautiful detail. This figurine was also made in smaller versions. *Author's collection. Photo by Laurie Morrison.*

A 12" Heubach boy figurine holding leaves. Circa 1910. *Courtesy of Christmas Archives International (U.K.) Ltd.*

Black boy figurine with ear of corn. 5¾"
high. Incised sunburst mark and #24.
*Collection of Shirley Lipnick. Photo by
Laurie Morrison.*

Chapter 4

Trinket Boxes/Dresser Boxes and Fairing Pieces

A number of lovely bisque and china boxes with removable lids decorated with children's heads or figurines were made by Gebruder Heubach and other German manufacturers. Examples also can be found that were made in England, France, the United States, and Japan.

These boxes had a variety of uses but primarily sat on a women's dresser and were used to hold jewelry, powder, and other articles. Collectors may come across lids without bottoms being sold for fairly hefty prices. In my opinion they don't have too much value as a collectible.

Heubach powder box made with the same head as a piano baby; approximately 8" high, bisque. *Illustration by Kathy Fable.*

These boxes date from the 1880s-1930s and were sometimes given away as prizes at fairs. Bisque and china figurines on a long base were also used for fair prizes and collectively these pieces became known as "fairing" pieces. The Strong Museum in Rochester, New York, has a quite wonderful collection of trinket boxes and fairing pieces.

Some of the manufacturers of trinket boxes and fairing pieces include
W. Goebel
Ernst Bohne
Karl Schneider
Alfred Voight
Gebruder Heubach.

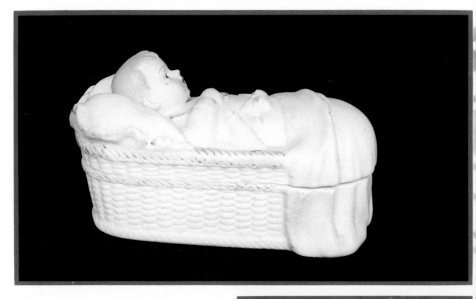

Trinket box with baby lying in cradle on top. 4½" long by 2¾" high. German, bisque, not marked. *Author's collection. Photo by Diane Freer.*

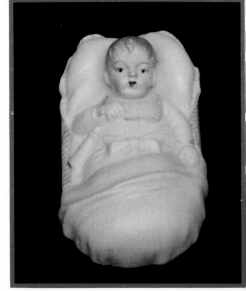

Trinket box with baby, front view.

China fairing piece. Dog and girl tugging doll in front of a fence. Gilt detail In black script in front of base it reads "Tug of War." Made by Conta & Boehm circa 1875. 2¾" high by 5¼" long. Incised "3336/43" on base. *Strong Museum, Rochester, New York.*

Kewpie trinket box, all bisque. 5" long figurine, 3⅞" high box. Goebel mark incised in base, "C" stamped on top, "Copyright Rose O'Neill" sticker on bottom. *Private collection.*

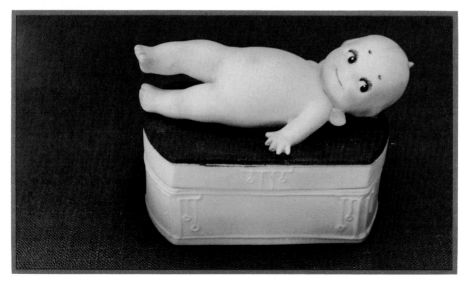

Trinket box with seated baby holding
gold rattle. German bisque, no marks.
4½" long by 4½" high. *Author's
collection. Photo by Diane Freer.*

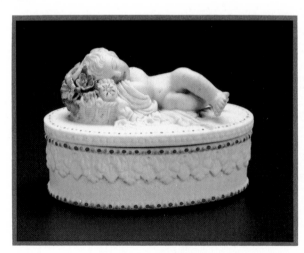

Parian trinket box with cherub lying on
blue blanket. Head resting on a basket
of flowers. Unusual American porcelain
example by U.S. Pottery of Bennington,
Vermont, circa 1850. 4⅞" long by 2⅞"
high. *Strong Museum, Rochester, New
York.*

Wonderful trinket box/fairing piece. Child on sideboard stealing grapes. Oval mirror in gold frame. China, circa 1880. *Strong Museum, Rochester, New York.*

Chapter 5

Figurines with Receptacles

Match Safes/Toothpick Holders/Vases/Planters

Children's figurines were an adornment for the home but often they were attached to a receptacle of some sort to make them functional as well. The most common types are match safes, toothpick holders, vases and planters. Often it is difficult to pinpoint which usage a piece was intended for and one can only deduce by the size and shape of the receptacle. As in any other type of figurine look for unusual pieces and good condition.

For marks that may be found on these pieces refer to the chapters on children figurines and Gebruder Heubach.

Two bisque boys with toothpick holders or match safes. The larger may be a planter. Boy in blue has gold trim and is of a very nice quality. He is 5¼" high. The boy in pink also has gold trim. The paper he is holding says "Our Best Congratulations" 7¼" high. Neither are marked but are of German quality. *Author's collection. Photo by Diane Freer.*

Opposite page:
Bisque boy dressed in early nineteenth century clothing with receptacle. Probably a match safe or toothpick holder. Decorated in pink with gold on the base. No marks. German. 6½" high. *Author's collection. Photo by Diane Freer.*

Bisque planter with boy's half-figurine set into it. 2½" high. No marks. *Author's collection. Photo by Laurie Morrison.*

Plump bisque girl with basket. Peach-
colored decoration with gold beading.
May have been meant as a planter or
toothpick holder. 5¾" high. *Author's
collection. Photo by Diane Freer.*

Young boy polishing a boot. May be a
toothpick holder. 3¾" high. *Author's
collection. Photo by Diane Freer.*

On left—German bisque girl with
receptacle, 5½" high and marked "64"
in blue. In the center is a piano baby
with her original mohair wig 3½" high.
On the right a German bisque girl with
a receptacle on the back. Unmarked,
5¼" high. *Collection of Jenny Jones.
Photo by Jim Yarbrough.*

Bisque boy with vase painted peach
with gold beading. Incised "43" on
bottom, 5¼" high. German. *Author's
collection. Photo by Diane Freer.*

61

Bisque girl holding up her dress; cat peaks through her feet and receptacle behind her, 2½" high. *Author's collection. Photo by Laurie Morrison.*

Cupid-type boy holding planter. China. Nice decoration; some damage. "52/122" on bottom. Probably Japanese. 6¼" high. *Author's collection. Photo by Diane Freer.*

Girl holding a dog with a receptacle behind her, 4¾" high.

Young musicians with planter. Not a very old piece. Incised "Made in Japan" on back and stamped "Made in Japan" in red ink on bottom. 4½" high. *Author's collection. Photo by Diane Freer.*

Boy and girl figurine planter. 4½" long by 3½" high. *Collection of Shirley Lipnick. Photo by Laurie Morrison.*

Chapter 6

Figurines from
Children's Book Illustrations

In the late nineteenth and early twentieth centuries, improved lithographic methods caused changes in book illustrations that were the basis for the growth of illustrated children's books. Many of the characters in the books became "the rage" much as movie and cartoon characters do today. Bisque figurines and other objects bearing the likeness of these characters became quite popular.

Kewpies, Kate Greenaway, and Sunbonnet Babies will be presented in the following pages. Other popular figurines were Palmer Cox's Brownies, which were gnomelike creatures and Mother Goose figurines.

Some examples of bisque Mother Goose figurines. German. *Collection of Daniel Jacoby. Photo by Laurie Morrison.*

Kate Greenaway Figurines

Kate Greenaway (1846-1901) was a well-known English illustrator of Christmas cards, children's books, and a series of almanacs. Her little girls wore empire style dresses with high waists and bonnets and the boys often wore hats, too. Her illustrations set styles for real children's clothes that were worn in several European countries. Ms. Greenaway's "children" were pictured on many items produced in Germany other than bisque figurines, including figural silver napkin rings, children's dishes, vases, and so forth.

Some of the figurines are very tiny, but they can also be found as large as eight inches.

Two small bisque figurines in their nightclothes. No marks. *Author's collection. Photo by Laurie Morrison.*

Kate Greenaway boy figurine writing on slate. 2½" high, all bisque, no marks, German. *Author's collection. Photo by Diane Freer.*

Small bisque girl with her arms around her legs. 1¼". No marks. *Author's collection. Photo by Laurie Morrison.*

Boy leaning on elbow with sweet face. German. 3½" long. No marks. *Author's collection. Photo by Diane Freer.*

Back view of boy leaning on elbow. Nice detail in the decoration.

Kate Greenaway stickers now being reproduced © Merrimack Publishing Corporation, New York, 1003. (Shown larger than actual size.) *Photo by Diane Freer.*

Tiny seated boy with a top hat, 1⅜"
high. *Author's collection.*

Girl in nightclothes leaning on elbow.
Bisque, 2⅛" long. *Author's collection.*
Photo by Laurie Morrison.

Bisque girl in nightclothes kneeling
and holding her night cap. 1½" high,
no marks. *Author's collection. Photo by
Laurie Morrison.*

Small girl in bonnet. Only 1" high.
Bisque, no marks. *Author's collection.*
Photo by Laurie Morrison.

Sunbonnet Babies

Bertha L. Corbett, a Minneapolis artist, published her first book, *The Sunbonnet Babies*, in 1900. The book featured fat children fully dressed with large bonnets that hid their faces. She created these characters to prove to a friend that a person can show "expression" without their face in view.

In 1902 *The Sunbonnet Primer* was published and Corbett also created several sets of prints of the Sunbonnet Babies. In addition to bisque figurines, postcards, valentines, decals, china items, and a tea set by Royal Bayreuth were produced. Royal Bayreuth recently issued plates with the Sunbonnet design on them.

Sunbonnet Baby bisque figurine bending over a washboard. Approximately 8" high. *Strong Museum, Rochester, New York.*

Sunbonnet Baby china by Royal
Bayreuth. All but a few pieces are of the
Sunbonnet Babies. *Photo courtesy of
James D. Julia, Inc.*

Sunbonnet Baby bisque figurine. Girl
in white bonnet, apron, and purple
dress holding rug beater in her right
hand and a rug in her left. Approximately
8" high. *Strong Museum, Rochester,
New York.*

Kewpies

Kewpies were the creation of author and artist Rose O'Neill and were so popular that literally hundreds of Kewpie items were created and are collected today. Kewpies first appeared in illustrations by Rose O'Neill in 1909 in the *Ladies Home Journal.* The Kewpies were modelled after O'Neill's little brother and in her imagination became the guardian angels for little children.

Kewpie figurines are bisque, primarily nude, somewhat unisex, and have molded hair in a "top knot." They have large painted side-glancing eyes, small blue wings at their neck, and starfish-shaped hands.

George Borgefeldt and Company of Berlin bought the rights to create the Kewpie figurines in 1912 and had them manufactured by various German porcelain companies for export to the United States. Originally J.D. Kestner and Company was designated as the manufacturer, but the demand was so great that many other manufacturers were needed to keep up the volume, including W. Goebel and Royal Rudolstadt.

Kewpies were also made in ceramic, plastic, rubber, cloth, composition and other materials. Both figurines and dolls with jointed limbs were created. The models for the figurines and dolls were actually sculpted by Joseph L. Kallus, a young art student at the time, who worked closely with Rose O'Neill.

In addition to figurines and dolls there are Kewpie dishes, handkerchiefs, perfume bottles, and other items. Many unauthorized versions of Kewpies have been made and Kewpie type figurines are still being produced today. Original bisque figurines were produced from 1912-1914 and again in the 1920s. (The hiatus was due to the First World War.)

Kewpie-type stickers sold in the B. Shackman store in New York, New York. © Merrimack Publishing Corporation, New York 10003. *Photo by Diane Freer.*

Two reproductions of Kewpie books currently being sold. *Photo by Diane Freer.*

Partial Kewpie tea set. Many different ones were manufactured. *Author's collection. Photo by Diane Freer.*

Kewpie "felts" which are part of a series. They were used to make small quilts for dolls. *Author's collection. Photo by Diane Freer.*

Kewpie needlework picture. *Collection of Rose Marie Willruth. Photo by Laurie Morrison.*

Ranging in size from ½ to 13 inches in height, with most between 2 and 5 inches, they originally sold for as little as 15 cents. Today quality examples sell for several hundred dollars.

The first Kewpies were rather static but as their popularity grew the "action" Kewpies were developed. The "action" Kewpies did things such as play the guitar, read, travel etc. They came in a variety of sizes and variations.

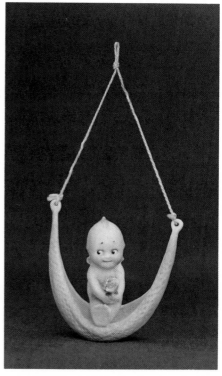

Kewpie inkwell. All bisque, 4¾" high overall, 3" high figurine. "O'Neill" incised; "46 29" incised, © stamp on bottom. *Private collection.*

Kewpie figurine in hammock. All bisque, 1⅞" high; stamped © on back. *Private collection.*

The action Kewpies received names from poems O'Neill wrote that appeared in the *Woman's Home Companion Magazine,* in which she called her Kewpies by such names as "Blunderbloo" (a Kewpie who was always tumbling), "The Huggers," "The Kewpie Reader," "Kewpie Traveller," "Sweeper," "Bookworm," and others. In addition, there are Kewpies that represent professions such as a gardener, soldier, lawyer, etc. Kewpies can also be found with various animals and objects (baskets, buckets, in a bed, etc.)

Also to be found in bisque are Kewpie match safes, toothpick holders, trinket boxes, salt and pepper shakers, vases, etc.

When buying Kewpie figurines it is desirable to find either the O'Neill signature incised on the foot or on the base or one of the original paper labels. Realistically, this is not always possible as many labels did not survive; therefore many Kewpies are now unmarked. Higher prices are commanded by unusual pieces and larger pieces, Kewpies with Doodle Dog (a black and white spotted dog), Kewpies with other objects, and Kewpies that are dressed.

Kewpie figurine in box with hinged arms (box does not open). All bisque, 4⅝" high. *Collection of Rose Marie Willruth. Photo by Laurie Morrison.*

In addition to Kestner, Goebel and Royal Rudolstadt, Kewpies were manufactured by Gebruder Voight, Hermann Voight, and many other companies. The Fritz Bierschenk Company made a business of dressing Kewpies manufactured by other porcelain manufacturers. Gebruder Heubach made Kewpie-like figurines and Louis Wolf and Co. of Germany made "chubbies." Chubbies had Kewpie-like faces and molded hair that came to a peak similar to the "topknot" of the Kewpies, but they were heavier and wore molded clothes.

Kewpies were also made by the Fulper Pottery Company of Flemington, New Jersey, in the 1920s. Japanese versions were made as late as the 1970s by the Lefton Co. and some imitations are being made in other parts of the Orient today.

Kewpies may carry the O'Neill signature incised in the foot of a figurine or on the base if the figure is sitting or reclining, or have one of several original paper labels. There were five different labels that appeared on the front of the figurine and three different copyright labels—usually found on the back of the figurine. They may also have a copyright mark © and various inventory numbers. Rare pieces may carry the Kestner crown mark or read "JDK." They may also be marked "Germany."

Japanese versions may be unmarked, carry paper labels, have inventory numbers on them, or read "Lefton Co."

O'Neill, J.D.K.

Kestner

Made in U.S.A.

Fulper

The International Rose O'Neill Club holds a Kewpiesta every April in Branson, Missouri, where Rose O'Neill lived. Collectors may also be interested in joining the Bonniebrook Historical Society which is rebuilding Rose O'Neill's home, which was burned to the ground several years ago. For information about membership in either of these organizations please refer to the back of this book.

Kewpie with guitar. Right foot incised "O'Neill," left foot stamped ©. 3⅝" high. *Private collection.*

"The Thinker" figurine—all bisque. Incised "O'Neill" on bottom. This one is 6¾" high; it also was made in 4¾" high and 4" high sizes. *Private collection.*

Three seated Kewpies, one with a butterfly on the head, another with a fly on its leg. All bisque, 4¼" high. *Collection of Rose Marie Willruth. Photo by Laurie Morrison.*

Kneeling bisque Kewpie. 4" high, stamped © on bottom. *Private collection.*

Bisque Kewpie with book. Copyright © stamped on bottom; 3¾" high. *Private collection.*

Kewpie at table having tea. Base carries Goebel mark, "déposé," "34," © stamped. Bisque, 4" high. *Private collection.*

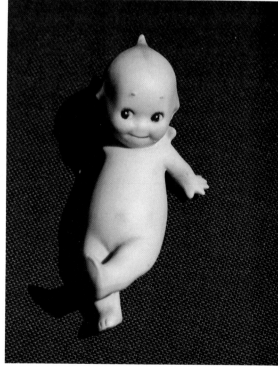

Sitting Kewpie with cat. Bisque, 3⅛" high, stamped or painted © on bottom. *Private collection.*

Bisque Kewpie lying on back. Incised "196 C," O'Neill, © stamped on. 4½" high. *Private collection.*

Black bisque Kewpie with hinged arms. Although this fellow is really a doll, he is included because black examples are rare. They were known as "Hottentots." Carries original Kewpie label—tiny Kewpie on string around his neck. 7" high. *Collection of Rosemarie Willruth. Photo by Laurie Morrison.*

A copy of a black bisque Kewpie made in the Orient. This reproduction is still being sold today by B. Shackman and Company in New York, New York. *Author's collection. Photo by Laurie Morrison.*

Bisque Kewpie policeman. No marks, 4" high. *Private collection.*

Three bisque Kewpie perfume bottles.
Large one stamped "O'Neill" on foot,
small ones say "Germany" on foot.
Large one is 3½" high, small ones are
3" high. *Collection of Rose Marie
Willruth. Photo by Laurie Morrison.*

Kewpie in wicker chair and Kewpie on
bench with Doodle Dog. Figure on
chair is 4½" high and has original
Kewpie label. The figure on the bench
is stamped ©. *Collection of Rose Marie
Willruth. Photo by Laurie Morrison.*

Kewpie Jasperware. *Photo courtesy Skinner's, Inc.*

Bisque Kewpie and swan. Paper label on figurine "Copyright Rose O'Neill." *Private collection.*

Tiny bisque Kewpie dressed in crepe paper. One of a dozen dressed in different outfits by Marshall Field's in Chicago for a customer's birthday cake. 1" high. *Author's collection. Photo by Diane Freer.*

Candy container with bisque Kewpie attached. Kewpie 5" high. *Collection of Rosemarie Willruth. Photo by Laurie Morrison.*

Three bisque, hinged-arm Kewpie dolls with molded clothing. Sailor boy with pants, signed "O'Neill" on foot, red label on front, 4⅞" high; sailor in shirt signed "O'Neill" in foot, 4¾" high; Kewpie with straw hat, signed "O'Neill" in foot, 4¾" high. *Collection of Rose Marie Willruth. Photo by Laurie Morrison.*

Bisque Kewpie lying on a trinket box. Stamped © on bottom, 1¾" high. *Private collection.*

Bisque Kewpie known as "The Traveller." Stamped ©, "O'Neill" incised in suitcase, "70" on right foot. 5" high. *Private collection.*

Leaping bisque Kewpie with glasses, 2¼" high. *Collection of Rose Marie Willruth. Photo by Laurie Morrison.*

Miniature bisque Kewpies—each represents a month of the year. No marks or labels, 1¾" high. *Private collection.*

Bisque Kewpie aviator. "Copyright Rose O'Neill" sticker on back. 3¾" high. *Private collection.*

Kewpie bride and groom. Bisque, 2½" high. Dressing Kewpies as a bride and groom was very popular. *Collection of Rose Marie Willruth. Photo by Laurie Morrison.*

Bisque Kewpies with matching chair and bench. Marked © on both pieces. Figure on bench 3¾" high, figure on chair 4" high. *Collection of Rose Marie Willruth. Photo by Laurie Morrison.*

Three bisque Japanese Kewpies—the "graduate" is stamped "05178" on bottom. Graduate: 4" high, Baby: 3" long, Nurse: 4" high. *Author's collection. Photo by Diane Freer.*

Two Kewpie bisque figurines believed to be Japanese but not marked. Figurine with finger in his mouth is 3½" high, Kewpie with bottle is 4½" high. *Author's collection. Photo by Laurie Morrison.*

A group of Japanese Kewpies. Clearly these can't be mistaken for the originals. *Author's collection. Photo by Laurie Morrison.*

Bisque Kewpie Huggers. No marks; probably Japanese. 4½" high. *Author's collection. Photo by Diane Freer.*

Kewpie soldier, all bisque. Label on back "Copyright Rose O'Neill." 4¾" high. *Private collection.*

Two bisque Kewpie Sweepers. The larger one is 4" high and has the original paper label on the front. The smaller one is 3½" high and is signed O'Neill in the foot. *Collection of Rose Marie Willruth. Photo by Laurie Morrison.*

Kewpie with Doodle Dog. All bisque, right foot stamped ©, left foot incised "O'Neill." 3½" high. *Private collection.*

Bisque Kewpie with no marks, probably Japanese. 5½" high. *Author's collection. Photo by Diane Freer.*

All-bisque Kewpie with basket. Stamped © on base. Incised "O'Neill." 4" high. *Private collection.*

Another version of a bisque Kewpie with a book, this one in a chair. Reads "Copyright Rose O'Neill" on cover of the book. Stamped © on bottom 3½" high. *Private collection.*

Place card holder/vase with Kewpie-related figurine. All bisque, believed to be one-of-a-kind. Incised "O'Neill." "47" incised in base of vase. 2½" total height, 1¾" height of figurine. *Private collection.*

Bisque Kewpie with mandolin in chair. Bottom of seat incised "10," stamped ©. 4" high overall, 2" high figurines. *Private collection.*

Blunderbloo Kewpie on sled. All bisque, © painted on bottom, "Copyright Rose O'Neill" sticker on back. Sled 2" long, overall 2" high. *Private collection.*

Chapter 7

Snowbabies and No-Snows

Snow babies are small figurines made of "hand-whipped" bisque and covered with a snowy-looking grout. Other authors have described them as "splattered with glitter sand," "in white pebble suits," and "with fired-on pebble texture clothing."

They range in size from about one-inch high to the snow baby dolls that can be as much as nine inches tall. They are found engaged in a variety of winter activities including skating, sledding, skiing, sitting on snowballs, and with polar bears.

There is a great controversy over the origin of snow babies. Most collectors, dealers, and authors say they were first manufactured any time from 1850-1890 and were originated from the sugar candy figurines colored with vegetable dyes and used to decorate Christmas cakes, trees, and displays. The alternative story is that snow babies were created as a commercial venture to capitalize on Peary and Cook's exploration of the North Pole. Credence is lent to this belief for several reasons. The first is that there exists a bisque group of men tugging on two sides of a globe in the snow-baby style. This figurine is featured on the cover of the Ray and Eilene Early's book *Snow*

Pointed hood snow baby, crawling, 3½" long. *Author's collection.*

Snow baby with sled. Stamped "Germany," 2" high. *Collection of Dorothy and Joe Haber.*

Snow baby straddling sled, 2¼" high, stamped "Germany" on bottom runner with unreadable incised numbers. *Author's collection. Photo by Diane Freer.*

Babies. The second reason to believe this origin is that Admiral Peary's wife published a book entitled *The Snowbaby* in 1901. It is most likely is that German manufacturers took the existing product and made it more salable by connecting it to Admiral Peary and the tremendous interest in his North Pole exploration.

In either case, by the 1890s the snow babies and related figurines—Santas, houses, churches, animals, birds, gnomes, polar bears, penguins, and others were being imported to England by the Tom Smith company, a cracker manufacturer and by the B. Shackman Company of New York, New York (an importer of fancy goods—toys, games, and novelties), and Sears and Roebuck to the United States. British cooks collected them to build elaborate displays on Christmas cakes.

After the First World War, not as many were imported to England due to anti-Germany sentiment, and the English made plaster of Paris copies until the mid-twentieth century. These have not survived very well. The German snow babies were not made much after the 1930s which is when the Japanese versions first appeared. There were some celluloid types as well. Snow babies made before 1891 are unmarked, but after 1891 they were marked "Made in Germany" by law. But during and after the First World War, when German goods were unpopular, shopkeepers sometimes removed the German mark and sold them as British or American products. Hence, 1930s snow babies could appear to be pre-1891 when they were actually made later. It is also possible that German manufacturers marked "Made in Germany" on the boxes rather than on the figurines, as most snow babies don't have a smooth area to mark unless they are sitting on a sled or other object.

The snow babies that are believed to date from the earliest period are the snow baby angels with pink wings. These are the most sought after by collectors and very hard to find. Bluish children with snowsuits are also from the early period, as are those with no detail in their mittens or shoes. They are more likely to be wearing hats, not hoods, with their hair exposed. Those with igloos, sleds, and skis tend to date from about 1910s-1920s; snow babies in hats, scarves, and caps are from the 1920s-1930s period. They range in size from about one to three inches tall, although larger examples are found. The larger ones may have been used as displays in shop windows. There are also rare snow baby dolls that have bisque heads, hands, and feet and cloth bodies. They can be eight inches tall or more.

Of interest to snow baby collectors as well are "no-snows." No-snows are bisque figurines that are identical versions of snow babies or a related subject without the snowy grout cover. They include gnomes, Santas, skating girls, igloos, penguins, bears, Dickensian figures, and others. They are about the same size as snow babies and are often painted in bright colors.

Snow babies were made by many German manufacturers, including
Hertwig and Company
Johann Moll
Heber and Company
Galluba and Hoffman
Wagner and Appel
Bahr and Proeschild
Christian Frederick Klurg
and Kley and Hahn
Gebruder Heubach probably made them as well.

Victorian snow baby ornament of cotton with scrap (paper) face covered with mica. Circa 1890s. *Collection of Dorothy and Joe Haber.*

Back-to-back snow babies on sled; 3"
high, 4" long. *Collection of Dorothy
and Joe Haber.*

Copies were made in Japan in the 1930s, again in the 1960s,
and more recently in Taiwan and Hong Kong. They originally
carried a paper label stating their origin, but that may no longer
exist.

In addition, there exists a small quantity of somewhat crude-
looking snow babies made of a porous chalklike substance in
the 1930s for B. Shackman and Company by a company in
Brooklyn, New York. These were made for Daniel Jacoby, B.
Shackman's grandson, to avoid having to buy German goods.
Unfortunately, this company could not compete with the
German porcelain manufacturer's artistry and the project was
abandoned. Sixteen different models were made.

Mr. Jacoby also experimented with phosphorescent paint on
some of the figurines to make them glow in the dark. There may
be a few rare examples of these which still can be found.

There are a number of other collectible items of interest to
snow baby collectors, which include Clapsaddle postcards
published in 1910 by the International Art Publishing Company,
books by Josephine Peary: *The Snow Baby, Children of the
Arctic, Snowland Folk* and a book by Marie Peary (Josephine's
daughter): *The Snowbaby's Own Story.* A Royal Bayreuth six-
piece tea set was also manufactured.

When purchasing snow babies, always check the condition;
some are quite dirty and they can't be cleaned. Many no-snows
have lost a great deal of their paint. Make certain the snow

A group of tiny snow babies including one on a polar bear and a snow elf. Two are marked "Germany." Sizes from left to right: 1⅜" high, 1" high, ⅝" high, ⅞" high, and 1⅜" high. *Collection of Dorothy and Joe Haber.*

The red sled brigade. The first snow baby is glued to his sled, the other three were molded together. Sizes from left to right: 1⅜" high, 1½" high, 1¾" high, and 1⅛" high. *Collection of Dorothy and Joe Haber.*

coverage is still fairly complete. Unless they are very unusual examples, poor condition lowers their value. Become familiar with the reproductions that are around to avoid paying top price for them.

Japanese reproductions in general have coarser snow or less snow coverage, the faces are crudely painted, sometimes even with Oriental eyes, and the painting is sloppier. If one style turns up very frequently, that can be a clue that they may not be very old. There were poor quality German examples made, too, so quality is not the only determination to a snow baby's origin. Some special features to look for are intaglio eyes, jointed arms and legs, wooden skis or a metal sled, souvenir markings, and match safe receptacle or pin cushion doll.

Look for those pieces stamped "Made in Germany," for that suggests the piece is not a reproduction. It is very rare to find a manufacturer's stamp on any of these figurines but if you do these are the ones you might find.

Snow baby marks

Hertwig

Baehr & Proeschild

Wagner & Apel

Heber & Co.

Galluba & Hoffman

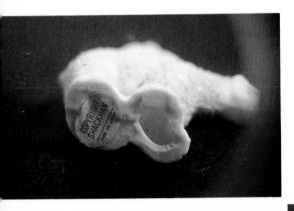

Example of a Shackman label on reproductions made in Japan.

"Germany" stamp on the bottom of a snow baby. *Photo by Laurie Morrison.*

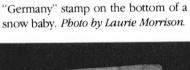

A group of snow babies, no-snows, and snow bears. *Photo courtesy of Skinner, Inc.*

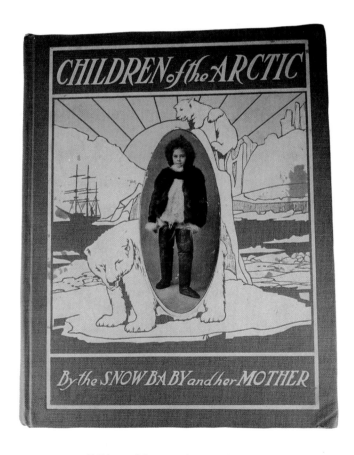

Children of the Arctic by Josephine and Marie Peary. *Author's collection. Photo by Diane Freer.*

Victorian Christmas cake exhibition piece decorated with 16 bisque snow babies and shoemaker elves. Central colored figure is German Christkind. Circa 1880. *Courtesy of The Christmas Archives International (U.K.) Ltd.*

Early German Christmas tree with "Christkind," similar to snow baby figurines. *Courtesy of The Christmas Archives International (U.K.) Ltd.*

A very rare "Cliquot Club" snow baby made by Heubach. It has an open section in the back that might have been a night-light or a vase. The snow baby has a large head and big side-glancing eyes. They appear to have been patterned after the children in the Cliquot Club Ginger Ale ads, although this has never been documented. Some black examples exist. *Illustration by Kathy Fable.*

Two original Cliquot Club Ginger Ale Ads. *Author's collection. Photo by Diane Freer.*

Snow babies on sleds

Three Japanese snow babies: 1⅝", ¾", and 1". *Collection of Dorothy and Joe Haber.*

No-snow boy and girl on sleds. Both stamped "Germany." 1½" long. *Collection of Linda Rehak and Andrew Swanson. Photo by Laurie Morrison.*

Two snow babies on sled together, both of very fine quality. *Collection of Rose Marie Willruth. Photo by Laurie Morrison.*

Large snow baby pushing small snow baby on sled. Stamped "Germany" and "5610" incised. *Author's collection. Photo by Diane Freer.*

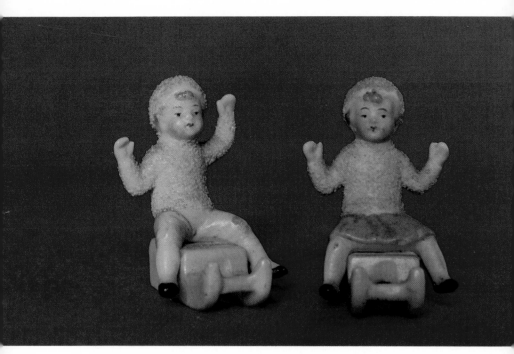

Boy and girl on sleds of very nice quality; 2¼" high. Incised "1768," stamped "Germany." *Author's collection. Photo by Diane Freer.*

A reproduction snow baby postcard. *Collection of Joyce Pimentel.* *Photo by Laurie Morrison.*

Two snow babies on sled ready to go downhill. Both stamped "Germany." 1¼" long and 2¼" long. *Collection of Joyce Pimentel. Photo by Laurie Morrison.*

One snow baby lying down and one sitting on sled; 2½" long, stamped Germany." *Collection of Linda Rehak and Andrew Swanson. Photo by Laurie Morrison.*

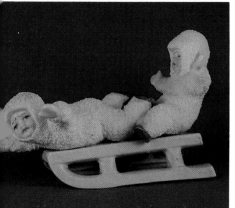

Sharing the sled. 4" long, stamped "Germany." *Collection of Linda Rehak and Andrew Swanson. Photo by Laurie Morrison.*

Snow babies with bears

Two versions of no-snows with bears stamped "Germany." 1¾" high. *Collection of Dorothy and Joe Haber.*

Japanese reproduction of a baby on a polar bear with two other babies. This group was sold as a set in the 1970s. 2⅞" high, 1¼" high, and 1" high respectively. Label on bottom reads "Copyright Shackman Made in Japan."

B. Shackman and Company originally imported snow babies from Germany and then later had them reproduced in the Orient. *Author's collection. Photo by Diane Freer.*

Baby on polar bear (2½" high) with
small bear beside it (1" high).
*Collection of Linda Rehak and Andrew
Swanson. Photo by Laurie Morrison.*

Three no-snow babies on grey snow
bear. No marks. 2¼" high. *Author's
collection. Photo by Diane Freer.*

Small snow baby and two small snow
bears. Bear on left ¾" high and 2¼"
long; bear on right ¾" high and 1½"
long. Figure is 1½" high. Small bear
stamped "Germany" on foot. *Author's
collection. Photo by Diane Freer.*

Large stuffed snow baby sold by B. Altman's, New York, for Christmas 1988 season. *Collection of Linda Rehak and Andrew Swanson. Photo by Laurie Morrison.*

No-snow children and no-snow bears bottle stoppers. *Collection of Linda Rehak and Andrew Swanson. Photo by Laurie Morrison.*

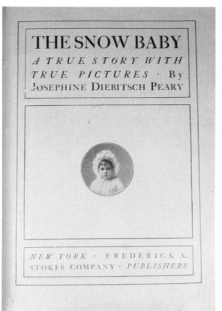

The front page of *The Snow Baby*, written by Marie Peary. *Author's collection. Photo by Diane Freer.*

Small snow baby candle holder, 1¼" high. *Collection of Dorothy and Joe Haber.*

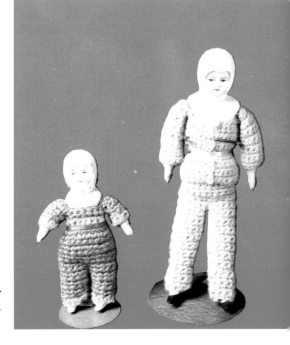

Two snow baby dolls with bisque heads, hands, and feet and cloth body, wearing crocheted clothes. These dolls are difficult to find but were made in a number of different sizes. These are 4½" high and 7" high. *Collection of Joyce Pimentel. Photo by Laurie Morrison.*

Original Clapsaddle postcards with snow babies. *Collection of Joyce Pimentel. Photo by Laurie Morrison.*

Snow babies with animals

Very sweet snow baby feeding a seal with a baby bottle. Stamped "Germany." 2" high. *Collection of Dorothy and Joe Haber.*

A Japanese version of a snow baby with a seal. Note the face and sloppy painting (red paint on ball runs onto face, too). This figurine can be found frequently. No marks. 2" high. *Author's collection. Photo by Laurie Morrison.*

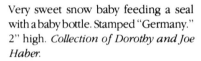

Snow baby pulling penguins on sled. Stamped "Germany" on bottom. 2¼" high. *Collection of Linda Rehak and Andrew Swanson. Photo by Laurie Morrison.*

Reindeer being driven by snow baby. No marks, 2" high by 3" long. *Collection of Linda Rehak and Andrew Swanson. Photo by Laurie Morrison.*

Snow babies standing up

These two snow babies are dancing; 1¾" high. The incised numbers on the bottom are not readable. *Collection of Linda Rebak and Andrew Swanson. Photo by Laurie Morrison.*

"Piggyback" on skis, 2½" high. *Collection of Linda Rebak and Andrew Swanson. Photo by Laurie Morrison.*

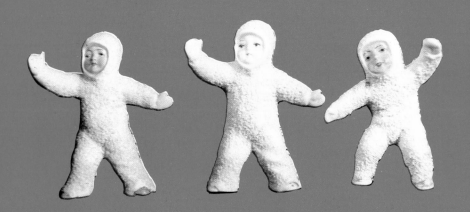

Three standing snow babies, 2¾" high. No marks. *Collection of Joyce Pimentel. Photo by Laurie Morrison.*

Larger standing snow babies, one on skis. Both 4" high; no marks. *Collection of Joyce Pimentel. Photo by Laurie Morrison.*

Snow babies in water globes made in the Orient for B. Shackman and Company in recent years. *Collection of Daniel Jacoby. Photo by Laurie Morrison.*

Snow baby twins

Snow baby reproductions being made in Hong Kong today. They are much larger than other snow babies (4"), have very scarce snow coverage, and have full faces with blue eyes. There is no mistaking them for the real thing. *Collection of Joyce Pimentel. Photo by Laurie Morrison.*

Snow baby twins with no marks, 2" high. *Collection of Dorothy and Joe Haber.*

"Snow suit twins" in original package. This no-snow reproduction was imported by B. Shackman and Company

from Japan. It was made in several different colors. *Collection of Daniel Jacoby. Photo by Laurie Morrison.*

No-snows

No-snow carolers. Look for this figurine with lantern intact; 3¾" high. Stamped "Germany" on back with incised number. *Collection of Joyce Pimentel. Photo by Laurie Morrison.*

Another group of no-snow Carollers. *Collection of Linda Rehak and Andrew Swanson. Photo by Laurie Morrison.*

Two children with bell (left) 2" high, stamped "Germany" and no-snow girl angel with santa (right). 1¾" high, stamped "Germany." *Collection of Linda Rehak and Andrew Swanson. Photo by Laurie Morrison.*

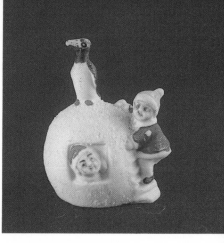

No-snow Santa with child in sled, 1½" high. *Collection of Dorothy and Joe Haber.*

No-snows in igloo with penguin, 1⅞" high. *Collection of Linda Rehak and Andrew Swanson. Photo by Laurie Morrison.*

Babies on hill with sled and baby (left), no marks, 2" high. No-snow Santa with 2 children (right), 2¼"high, stamped "Germany." *Collection of Linda Rehak and Andrew Swanson.*

One snow baby and two no-snows making a pyramid, 2" high. This is one of the figurines that was imported from Germany by B. Shackman and Company and then later reproduced by them. This one is not marked. *Collection of Linda Rehak and Andrew Swanson. Photo by Laurie Morrison.*

Snow baby in Christmas tree ornament egg. Made in the Orient and imported by the B. Shackman and Company in recent years. *Collection of Daniel Jacoby. Photo by Laurie Morrison.*

Snow boy skier with wooden skis and metal pole (one pole missing), 5½" high. *Collection of Linda Rehak and Andrew Swanson. Photo by Laurie Morrison.*

No-snow skater and children on sleds. One stamped "Germany." From left to right: 2" high, 1¾" high, and 1¼" high. *Collection of Dorothy and Joe Haber.*

Four examples of the rubber mold snow babies manufactured for the B. Shackman and Company. *Collection of Daniel Jacoby. Photo by Laurie Morrison.*

Two penguins on a snow slope, 2¾"
high. Reproduced and imported from
Japan by B. Shackman and Company.
*Collection of Daniel Jacoby. Photo by
Laurie Morrison.*

A highly rare black snow baby. It
appears to be original but there is no
documentation about black snow
babies other than the Cliquot type. The
feet were once painted brown but are
now chipped. They appear to have
been a different shade of brown than
the figurine's face. 2" high. *Author's
collection. Photo by Laurie Morrison.*

Two snow children sliding down a
wall; both 2¼" high. Stamped
"Germany" on the bottom. This
figurine was imported by B. Shackman
and Company from Germany and then
later reproduced by them of "imitation
china," according to their literature.
*Collection of Linda Rehak and Andrew
Swanson. Photo by Laurie Morrison.*

This seated baby appears to be the
white version of the black snow baby
previously pictured. They have the
same pose, mittened hands, and brown
shoes. 2¼" high. *Author's collection.
Photo by Diane Freer.*

117

Lazy snow babies

Three seated snow babies, 2¼" high. *Collection of Joyce Pimentel. Photo by Laurie Morrison.*

These two snow babies look surprised, as if they have just been hit with a snowball. 1¾" high (seated) and 2½" high (standing). *Collection of Dorothy and Joe Haber.*

Small seated snow baby with a cute face, 1" high. *Collection of Dorothy and Joe Haber.*

Boy and girl snow baby with lovely faces, 1¾" high. *Collection of Linda Rehak and Andrew Swanson.*

Detail of snow girl from back. Even on such a small figurine her "pantaloons" are wonderfully detailed. This type of attention to detail is the sign of a quality manufacturer—perhaps Heubach. *Photo by Laurie Morrison.*

Four little snow babies doing their tumbling act. The second figurine is marked "Germany." From left to right: 1⅝" high, 1⅛" high, ⅝" high, and 1" high. *Collection of Dorothy and Joe Haber.*

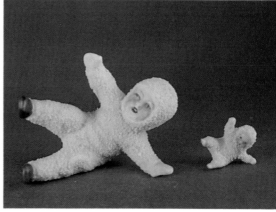

Two snow babies leaning on their sides. The tiny one is stamped "Germany"; 2" high and ¾" high. *Collection of Linda Rehak and Andrew Swanson. Photo by Laurie Morrison.*

Snow babies with snow balls

The boxed set of snow babies, including two on snowballs, is being reproduced in the Orient today for B. Shackman and Company. However, a saleswoman in their store told me they would not be continuing the line as it has become too expensive to reproduce. *Author's collection. Photo by Laurie Morrison.*

The snow baby on top of the snow ball is 2½" high. The no-snow pushing the snow ball is 2" high. *Collection of Joyce Pimentel. Photo by Laurie Morrison.*

Snow girl skater, 2" high. *Author's collection. Photo by Diane Freer.*

Two snow babies planting the U.S. flag on the North Pole. Hole in back of figurine for use as a planter. Incised "Germany" on the bottom; 3" high. *Collection of Linda Rehak and Andrew Swanson.*

Snow baby with guitar or mandolin and snow baby with tennis racket (anyone for tennis in the snow?). Both 2⅞" high. *Collection of Joyce Pimentel. Photo by Laurie Morrison.*

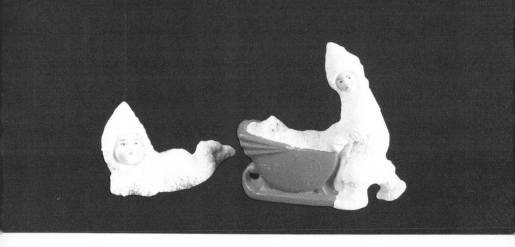

Charming pointed hood snow babies. The one lying down has a very nice face (2¼" long by 1¼" high) and the mother strolls with her twins in a combination baby carriage/sled. The mother is 2½" high and incised "7166" on back. She has all snow feet (no shoes). Both German. *Collection of Joyce Pimentel. Photo by Laurie Morrison.*

Reproductions

Left and above:
These reproduction snow babies are currently being made in Hong Kong. There seem to be different figurines each Christmas. In addition to those shown, there are snow baby angels playing instruments. They are sold in retail stores and by mail order. In no way do they attempt to confuse the collector. They are much larger than the old snow babies and have wide faces and blue eyes. The bisque has a yellowish tint to it. They are 4" or more in height but also much bulkier. *Collection of Joyce Pimentel and author. Photos by Laurie Morrison.*

123

Three snow babies from Japan, measuring 2", 1⅞", and 2" high. *Collection of Joe and Dorothy Haber.*

Rare snow baby with jointed arms and legs, 3½" high. German. *Collection of Linda Rehak and Andrew Swanson. Photo by Laurie Morrison.*

Chapter 8

Frozen Charlottes/Charleys or Bathing Dolls

Also known as Bething Babies, Swimming Dolls, Pillar Dolls, Solid China Dolls, Teacup Dolls, Penny Dolls

Although often called dolls, Frozen Charlottes meet my criteria for being a figurine (they have no hinged parts, hair is molded and painted on, and they had many uses).

Frozen Charlottes (this term will be used for simplicity hereafter, but it includes the male version: Frozen Charleys) are bisque or china figurines that were made by the thousands by German porcelain manufacturers. They were manufactured from the mid-nineteenth century until as late as 1940 in some German porcelain manufacturing companies. They were made in female and male versions that are differentiated only by their hairstyles in black or blonde molded or painted-on hair (Very unusual examples may wear a mohair wig.) The china Charlottes tend to have black hair, while the stone bisques tend to have blonde. Even in the later figurines, the hairstyles are those of the 1840s-1870s.

Their faces are painted on and the eyes are blue, brown, or gray. They may be of a white bisque, a tinted bisque, or a combination of both. Most Frozen Charlottes are naked, with the more unusual examples having one or more garments molded

Six small Frozen Charlottes, the second and third from the left are bisque while the others are china. Note that some have nicely detailed faces and others are very crude. In the Carl Stirn catalog of *1893* similar dolls sold for 90¢ per *gross* wholesale! 1 to 1½″ high. *Author's collection. Photo by Diane Freer.*

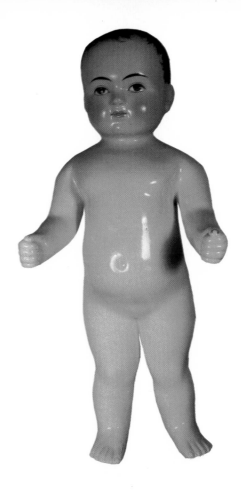

Large dark-haired Frozen Charley with tinted bisque face, white bisque body; 14½" high. *Collection of Rose Marie Willruth. Photo by Laurie Morrison.*

Fair Charlotte

Fair Charlotte lived on a mountain side,
In a wild and lonely spot,
No dwelling was three miles 'round
Except her father's cot.

On many a cold and wintry night,
Young swains were gathered there,
For her father kept a social board,
And she was very fair.

Her father loved to see her dress
Fine as a city belle—
She was the only child he had
And he loved his daughter well.

On New Year's Eve when the sun was set,
She gazed with a wistful eye
Out of the frosty window forth,
To see the sleighs go by.

She restless was and longing looked
Till a well-known voice she heard,
Came dashing up to her father's door—
Young Charlie's sleigh appeared.

Her mother said, "My daughter dear,
This blanket 'round you fold,
For 'tis an awful night without,
And you'll be very cold."

"Oh nay, oh nay," young Charlotte cried,
And she laughed like a Gypsy queen,
"To ride in a blanket muffled up,
I never will be seen."

My woolen cloak is quite enough,
You know it is lined throughout,
Besides I have my silken shawl,
To tie my neck about."

Her gloves and bonnet being on
She jumped into the sleigh,
And off they went down the mountainside
And over the hills away.

With muffled faces, silently,
Five long cold miles were passed,
When Charles in few and broken words,
The silence broke at last.

"Oh! such a night I never saw,
My lines I scarce can hold,"
Fair Charlotte said, in a feeble voice,
"I am exceedingly cold."

He cracked his whip and they onward sped,
Much faster than before,
Until five other dreary miles,
In silence they passed o'er.

"How fast," said Charles, "the frozen ice
Is gathering on my brow,"
Said Charlotte in a weaker voice,
"I'm growing warmer now."

Thus on they went through the frosty air,
And in the cold starlight,
Until the village and bright ballroom,
They did appear in sight.

Charles drove to the door, and jumping out,
He held his hand to her,
"Why sit you like a monument,
That has no power to stir?"

He asked her once, he asked her twice,
She answered never a word;
He asked her for her hand again,
But still she never stirred.

Black china Frozen Charlotte, 3½" high.
Author's collection. Photo by Diane Freer.

He took her hand into his own,
Oh God! it was cold as stone!
He tore her mantle from her brow,
On her face the cold stars shone.

Then quickly to the lighted hall,
Her lifeless form he bore,
Fair Charlotte was a frozen corpse,
And her lips spake never more.

He threw himself down by her side,
And bitter tears did flow,
And he said, "My own, my youthful bride,
I never more shall know!"

He bore her body to the sleigh,
And with it he drove home,
And when he reached her father's door,
Oh! How her parents mourned!

They mourned the loss of a daughter dear,
And Charles mourned o'er her doom,
Until at last his heart did break,
And they both lie in one tomb.

Back view of black china Frozen Charlotte. Note the spots where the glaze is missing and the white bisque shows through. It is common to find these figurines with this blemish, which was made in the manufacturing process and is not damage from a later date.

China Frozen Charlotte with sweet face, blue eyes. 4½" high. *Author's collection. Photo by Diane Freer.*

and painted on. They generally range in size from one-half inch to almost twenty inches in length. The more rare examples are black and Oriental Charlottes.

It is not unusual to find a spot on the back of a china Frozen Charlotte that is unglazed, for this was probably made when the figurine was laid down to dry after glazing. Additionally, some may have a round hole in the bottom of their torso, which is a pouring hole that was created during manufacturing.

Tiny Frozen Charlottes tend to have their arms "frozen" at their sides or across their chests, while the larger ones have these positions as well as arms outstretched in front of them. Some also have clenched fists. Rare versions may have hinged arms, but the legs were made joined or separated but never jointed. As with snow babies, small Frozen Charlottes were probably used as Victorian cake decorations and as charms in Christmas puddings. The tiniest ones were no more than one-half to one inch long, were very crude in appearance, and were clearly novelties. These are the ones that were also used for doll house babies and were often called penny dolls. A story is also told that they were served with tea and used as stirrers. If they cracked from the heat of the tea, no one cared because the replacement cost was so small.

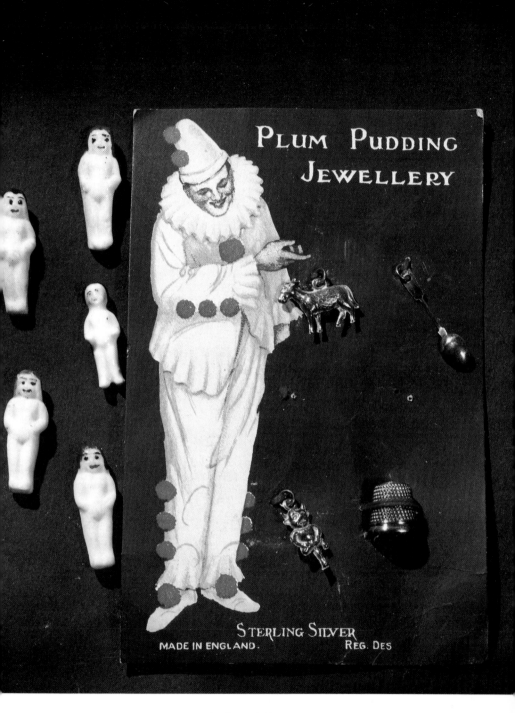

Tiny Frozen Charlotte dolls were used
as Christmas pudding charms. *Courtesy
of Christmas Archives International
(U.K.) Ltd.*

Small Charlottes were also used as wedding trinkets (to suggest fertility) and as christening trinkets.

Some other unusual examples that can be found in the Strong Museum in Rochester, New York, are bisque whistles with Frozen Charlottes on them and Charlottes encased in blown glass, much like a ship in a bottle.

Because of the way their arms are frozen in position, this story has been circulated about their origin. In the early nineteenth century there was a young girl named Charlotte whose mother had made her a new coat. Charlotte's beau came to call and take her on a sleigh ride, and her mother told her to wear her new coat. Rebelling as all teenagers do, Charlotte merely wrapped her shawl around her shoulders and went on her way. When they reached their destination, her boyfriend was astonished to find she had frozen with her arms extended at her side. Hence the name "Frozen Charlotte" used to explain the immovable arms and the "dead-white" pallor of these figurines.

This story was more than likely "lifted" from a popular American Folk ballad "Fair Charlotte," written by an wandering song writer named Carter in 1833. As it was circulated numerous versions appeared in different states. The Vermont version is included at the beginning of this chapter.

In Germany, where these figurines were produced, they were known as bathing dolls (*badekinder*) or swimming dolls. They were used by children at play during the summer months at the beach. The best quality of them would "swim" horizontally on the surface of the water; the poorer quality were more vertical when placed in the water.

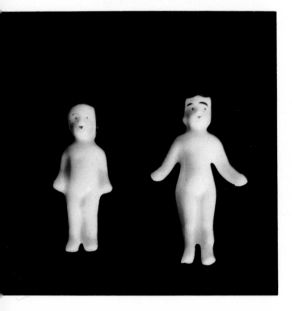

Two china Frozen Charlottes. Notice how different the body shapes are since each manufacturer had his own style. Figure on left 1¾" high, on right 2¼" high. *Author's collection. Photo by Diane Freer.*

Early china Biedermeier doll (from 1820s-1850s) with original wig and clothing. This doll has a less severe look than a Frozen Charlotte, but I feel there is a relationship between them. *Author's collection. Photo by Laurie Morrison.*

A stone bisque Frozen Charley with gold boots; a rather strange-looking fellow. 3¼" high. *Author's collection. Photo by Diane Freer.*

A reproduction of the 15½-inch Frozen Charley was made in the 1970s in Germany that looks almost identical to the original and is not marked as a reproduction.

Features that indicate a premium price include a pink tint to the bisque, unusual decoration such as molded clothing, an other-than-ordinary hair style, original clothing made for the figurine, jointed arms, black or Oriental appearance, a Charlotte in an egg or bathtub, or anything else unusual. Simon and Halbig made bathing dolls with elaborate hair styles and glass eyes that are quite valuable.

When buying Frozen Charlottes look for the highest quality, good molding, and more-detailed figurines. The bisque ones tend to be more crude than the china. Avoid repairs, chips, and cracks.

Many German manufacturers listed bathing dolls in their inventory. These include

Conta and Boehme
C.F. Kling
Max Buchold
August Riedeler
Alt, Beck, Gottschalck
Baehr & Proeschild
Simon and Halbig
Gebruder Beck and Glaser
Bernhardt & Bauer
S. Bertram
J.C. Sohn A.G.
Bloedner
Theodor Buschbaum
Johann Christian Eberlan
Rudolph Forster

Otto Gans
George Herbert
W. Goebel
Carl Hein
Hertel Schwab & Company
Hertwig & Company
Ernst Heubach
Julius Heubach
J.D. Kestner
A.W. Fr. Kister
Kohl and Wegenroth
Gebruder Kuhnlenz
Leube & Company
and Theodor Pohl.

Marks: Few of these figurines are signed, but some are known to be signed by Conta and Boehme (their Charlottes often had a hole through their clenched fists) and C.F. Kling. Some Frozen Charlottes are marked "Germany" or have mold numbers.

August Riedler

Ernst Bohne

Baehr & Proeschild

C.F. Kling

Conta & Boehm

This Charlotte is damaged, but it is included because the face is so poorly painted that it is an example of how quality may vary. *Author's collection. Photo by Diane Freer.*

Unusual Frozen Charley in striped boxer shorts with gold bow. White with black molded hair. *Strong Museum, Rochester, New York.*

Three frozen Charlottes that have dresses. The large blonde Charlotte is very desirable for its hair color and molded clothing. The other two Charlottes are appealing in their homemade dresses. The largest in the middle is 4¾" high, the one on the left is 3¾" high, and the one on the right is 2¼" high. *Author's collection. Photo by Laurie Morrison.*

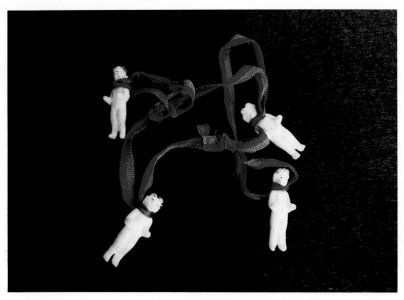

A group of little Frozen Charlottes strung together long ago on a Christmas ribbon. 1 to 1¼" high. These very little ones originally sold for 1¢ and were bought in candy stores by little girls. They were called "penny dolls." *Author's collection. Photo by Diane Freer.*

Very unusual "basket" of Frozen Charlottes. "The Old Woman Who Lived in the Shoe" is depicted with ten small Frozen Charlottes, circa 1890. *Strong Museum, Rochester, New York.*

Collection of Frozen Charlottes purchased in an old Christmas box. The tiny Charlottes at the top are hanging from a pair of china shoes that were imported from Germany by B. Shackman and Company to use as wedding cake decorations. The bottom row consists of a bisque dancing girl that is not a Frozen Charlotte, a bisque egg with a tiny Frozen Charlotte sitting in it, and two tiny snow babies. *Author's collection. Photo by Diane Freer.*

Large china Frozen Charley with blonde hair and blue eyes, 9" high. Lightly tinted face and all-white body. *Collection of Rose Marie Willruth. Photo by Laurie Morrison.*

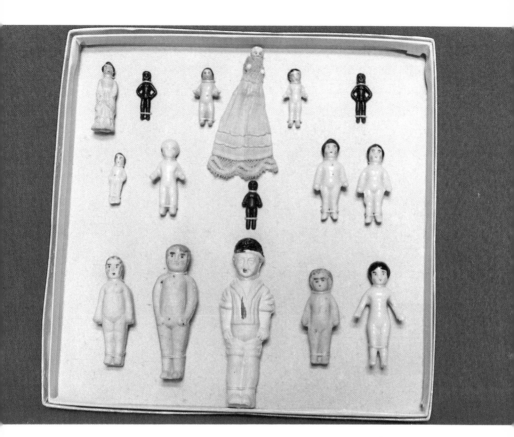

This collection of Frozen Charlottes was purchased the same time as the collection in the Christmas box and may have come out of the same attic. It includes bisque and china Charlottes, a figure in a long white dress, and a tiny baby in a long christening dress, circa 1880. *Author's collection. Photo by Diane Freer.*

Group of Frozen Charlottes with black and pink skin tone, china. *Collection of Jenny Jones. Photo by Jim Yarbrough.*

Frozen Ch
(bathing ch
made from
moving joi
half inch to
were small
and be pur
produced i

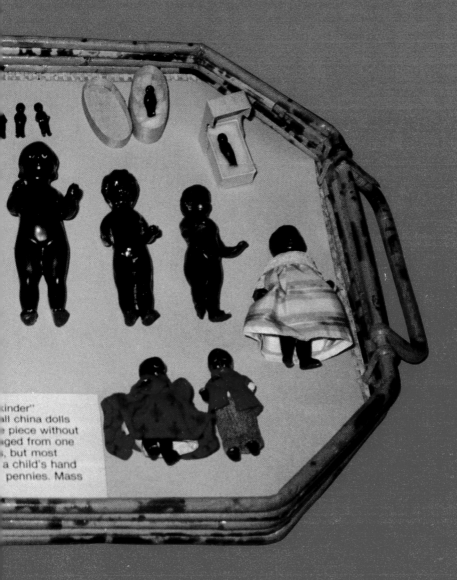

...kinder"
...all china dolls
...e piece without
...ged from one
...s, but most
...a child's hand
...pennies. Mass

Collection of black Frozen Charlottes/
Charleys of many sizes. *Collection of
Jenny Jones.*

Rare Oriental Frozen Charley, china
with molded skull cap and blue tunic,
5" high. *Strong Museum, Rochester,
New York.*

Chapter 9
Immobiles and Character Figurines

Immobiles are small bisque figurines that stand straight with their hands at their sides and are not engaged in any activity. Created in the 1920s and 1930s, they have molded clothes and hair and their decoration, which is unfired, wears off easily.

Many of the immobiles were made as comic and cartoon characters. An early B. Shackman catalog (U.S. importers of "fancy" goods) includes comic sets from *Orphan Annie*, *The Gumps*, and *Our Gang*—all of which have children figurines included in them. They also came as complete families (parents and two children) and are sometimes still found in original boxes.

Flapper style bisque immobile, circa 1920. Paint pretty worn, foot chipped which is not an uncommon condition to find immobiles in. No marks. 3¾" high. *Author's collection. Photo by Diane Freer.*

Bisque Oriental girl with umbrella, 4" high. Stamped "Made in Japan" on bottom. *Author's collection. Photo by Diane Freer.*

Immobile boy in red short pants outfit. Bisque, 2½" high. Marked "Germany," "178 " on back. *Collection of Daniel Jacoby. Photo by Laurie Morrison.*

Flapper girl immobile holding a ball from the 1920s. Decoration somewhat worn. Incised "0317" on back. 5" high. German. *Author's collection. Photo by Diane Freer.*

Immobiles, which were originally used for party favors and given as prizes at fairs, can be quite charming and relatively inexpensive to collect. Look for good body condition, nice detail, and paint in good condition.

The better-quality versions were made in Germany, yet Japan made copies as well.

Marks:

May be stamped or incised "Germany" on back. Sometimes the name of the character is incised as well. They may also be marked "Made in Japan." Older pieces might be marked "Nippon" (Japan) and therefore are more valuable. Many were made by Hertwig & Company.

Hertwig

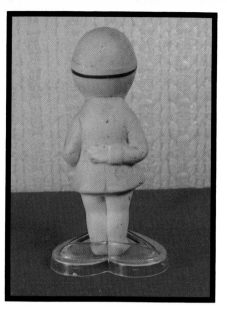

Boy with goggles, circa 1920. *Collection of Rose Marie Willruth. Photo by Laurie Morrison.*

Small standing girl, marked "Japan" in black, 3½" high.

Cowboy and Cowgirl immobile figurines. Stamped "Made in Japan" on bottom. Nice decoration, small chip in base of cowgirl; 4" high. *Author's collection. Photo by Laurie Morrison.*

Chapter 10
Nodders and Swayers

Nodders are figurines with heads that move that were used in China centuries ago as temple figurines of gods. The Meissen porcelain company of Germany and a number of French porcelain manufacturers in the eighteenth century and early nineteenth century made them based on the Chinese designs.

In the later nineteenth century the nodding concept was applied to dolls made with a mechanism to nod the head by pushing on the chest. These dolls were made to give a child a sense of interaction with the doll.

The nodders of interest to children figurine enthusiasts were made of bisque in the 1920s and 1930s in Germany. Some nodders are similar to immobile figurines except that they have an elastic string through them to allow their heads to be tipped forward, backward, or sideways. In this type of figurine the name "nodder" seems a misnomer—the head will not "bob" as the name suggests.

A "swayer" type girl on cone-shaped base holds two cats in her arms and is marked on the base, "What if I am fat? I have a loving disposition." All bisque, 3¾", incised "8654," and marked with a star with crown (could be the Kestner mark). Also marked "Made in Germany."

B. Shackman and Company had the same figurine in their catalog of imported items from Germany around 1910-1920, but she is described as a "comic china figure." *Collection of Shirley Lipnick. Photo by Laurie Morrison.*

Bisque girl holding a female and male doll in each hand, incised "Germany." *Strong Museum, Rochester New York.*

Baby girl wrapped in bunting bisque nodder; head nods front to back; German. *Strong Museum, Rochester, New York.*

Other types of nodders are attached to a wire that allows them to move up and down quite freely after being touched, or have a metal bar with a weight in them that allows their heads to rock. Yet others have heads that fit over a cone-shaped bisque base that allows them to sway or rock, and these are sometimes called "swayers."

Three comic figurine nodders. Note the knot from the elastic at the top of their heads. Figure on the left is "Smitty," 3½" high; middle is "Orphan Annie," 3¼" high; on the right is "Chester Gump," 2½" high. All bisque and stamped "Germany" on back. *Collection of Daniel Jacoby. Photo by Laurie Morrison.*

Bisque nodder girl with gold purse—elastic strung type. 4" high, incised "Germany" on back. *Author's collection. Photo by Diane Freer.*

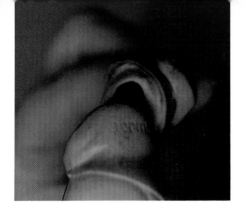

Detail of nodder girl showing how elastic is strung to head and "Germany" mark.

Nodders, like immobiles, are often comic characters and are frequently found with the paint worn off. They were also made of celluloid, composition, and other materials. Nodder animals were made as well.

Modern versions of nodders are those bobbing figures you might see in the back of a car and sports figures with large heads made in Japan.

Marks:

One of the major manufacturers of nodders was Hertwig & Co. whose mark is shown here. However, it is unlikely to find a signed piece. Nodders may be marked "Germany."

Hertwig

Two more comic figure nodders: "Kayo" and "Herbie," both 2¼" high. "Made in Germany" on back. *Collection of Daniel Jacoby. Photo by Laurie Morrison.*

A family affair. An unusual group of nodders—mother, father, one child standing and two sitting. Made by Ernest Bohne, Germany, 1854. *Strong Museum. Rochester, New York.*

Chapter 11

Half Dolls or Half-Figurines

Also Known as Pin Cushion Dolls, Tea Cozy Dolls, Busts, Tea Busts, Tea Warmers, *Teepupenkoffe, Tetes por Cosets,* Dresser Dolls, Whiskbroom Dolls, Tops, Pin Heads.

Half-figurines or half-dolls predominantly represent women, but a resourceful collector can find many children half-figurine examples. Even Kewpie and Frozen Charlotte half-figurines exist.

Half-dolls are either a head or a head and body to the waist which had a very full skirt attached to it at one time. Few of the original skirts have survived. They once sat on top of a pin cushion, powder box, or clothes brush on a woman's dresser. They were also used to cover tea pots, as hat pin holders, and attached to pillows.

Half-dolls were made from the mid-nineteenth century until the first half of the twentieth century, but they were most popular from about 1900 to 1925.

The figurines have holes in the bottom to which the skirt was attached. Some are nude, others have painted clothing. The arms may be outstretched, at the figurine's side, or folded, etc.

Young girl with hands together marked "Germany," 1¾" high. *Author's collection. Photo by Laurie Morrison.*

Young girl half-doll of bisque with
blonde hair holding a doll in her hand.
Incised "Germany" #22289."
Approximately 2½" high. *Strong
Museum, Rochester, New York.*

Girl in Dutch cap clutching flower, 2¼" high. Marked "Made in Germany" and "5237." *Photo by Laurie Morrison.*

Made of china or bisque, these half-figurines were manufactured primarily in Germany by such companies as
W. Goebel
Dressel and Kister
J.D. Kestner
Limbach
Schneider
Royal Rudolstadt
Else Arrenberg
Bauer and Richter
Galluba and Hoffman
Hertel, Schwab and Company
Gebruder Heubach
Eugen Hommel
and August Riedler.
Fulper Potteries in the United States also made them for a short while around the time of the First World War. The Japanese copied them as well in the early part of the century, and reproductions are being made in Taiwan today—most of these reproductions have their arms at their sides.

Half-figurines were made in literally hundreds of different poses, and subjects with sizes ranging from one to nine inches in height.

In her book *All-Bisque and Half-Bisque Dolls*, Genevieve Angione refers to dolls that are bisque to the waist, have cloth bodies, and bisque feet as "half-dolls." She calls a half-figurine a "pincushion top." Although "half-doll" is the commonly used term for these half-figurines today, there may be some confusion with Angione's use of the term "half-doll."

The most valued half-figurines are those of high quality, the more elaborate or detailed pieces. If possible buy a piece with the skirt still attached. Look for signed pieces, those marked "Germany," and the unusual examples.

Marks:

Although a good number are unmarked by the manufacturer, many pieces have an inventory or mold number. Signed pieces are the most valuable. After 1891, German goods for export were marked "Germany," but the mark may have been merely stamped and now has worn off. Many pieces have "Germany" incised in them.

F. & W. Goebel

DEP

Karl Schneider

Dressed & Kister
(Other variations exist)

RW

August Riedler

AR

Royal Rudolstadt

Heubach
Sunburst
Mark

Limbach

Other
Heubach
Marks

J.D. Kestner

Galluba & Hoffman

HEU:
BACH

Heubach
Square
Mark

Half-doll/figurine marks. Many may never be seen on the figurines, but I provide them "just in case."

Girl with blonde "banana" curls, 2¼" high. Marked "Made in Germany," also numbers are incised that are unreadable. *Author's collection. Photo by Laurie Morrison.*

Young girl holding posies, 2½" high, marked "Made in Germany." *Author's collection.*

Examples of fairy tale figurines may be found on half or whole figurines used as clothes brush tops. This illustration shows "Gretel" of Hansel and Gretel. *Illustration by Kathy Fable.*

Unusual boy in school uniform with strangely pursed lips approximately 6" high. *Strong Museum, Rochester, New York.*

Chapter 12

Leakers or Naughty Figurines

Primarily made in Germany, it would appear from comparison with other German bisque pieces that these figurines were made in the late nineteenth to early twentieth century. They are small figurines (most are 1¾ to 2¼ inches in height) that are hollow inside and have holes in their heads that once held a rubber stopper.

Randy Selnick, a collector of these figurines, shares two explanations regarding their original use. The first is that they were perfume bottles, and the second is that they were used in men's clubs to put out burning cigar stubs. Perhaps they were simply novelty items. It's unlikely to find one with the stopper still intact. Many are signed "Germany."

Three male figurines which are remarkably similar. All bisque. Japanese versions of this figure exist. They are bulkier and stamped "Made in Japan" on the foot. *Collection of Randy Selnick.*

In addition to the sweet children shown here, there are naughty bottles with woman figurines in rather risqué poses. They might be called (with some poetic license) "risqué bisque." Most of these bottles are made of bisque, but some metal examples exist as well.

Two young girl figurines seated on "pottys," a common theme in German child figurines. Note the dog peeking through one girl's legs. All bisque. *Collection of Randy Selnick.*

Some more unusual examples of naughty bottle figurines. A cupid-type, a figure dressed as a soldier, and one that is clothed but with bare feet. All bisque. *Collection of Randy Selnick.*

An unusual black naughty bottle, the more common type in the middle and a boy with a rakish hat. The black figurine is china and bisque, the other two all bisque. *Collection of Randy Selnick.*

Two children looking at the floor— one with a very odd expression. All bisque. *Collection of Randy Selnick.*

The figurine on the left is made of some sort of metal, the one in the middle is unusually small. *Collection of Randy Selnick.*

Chapter 13

Occupied Japan

To help restore the economy in Japan after World War Two, Japanese pottery companies manufactured thousands of figurines and other decorative items that were exported primarily to the United States. During the American Occupation from 1945 until its end on April 18, 1952, one of the following marks was required to be stamped on the bottoms of these pieces: "Made in Japan," "Japan," "Made in Occupied Japan," or "Occupied Japan." The pieces that are specifically of interest in this group are labelled "Occupied Japan" or "Made in Occupied Japan," as the other marks were also used in other time periods. While figurines were among the first to interest collectors, many other types of Occupied Japan items are now sought after as well.

Girl holding staff with dog. China, 4¼" high. Marked "Made in Occupied Japan" stamped in black ink. *Author's collection. Photo by Diane Freer.*

Occupied Japan figurines of children include porcelain fish bowl items (they were made to hold fishing poles which may now be missing), planters, salt and pepper shakers, toothpick holders and bud vases with children figurines attached, bisque single figurines and pairs of figurines, and bisque and china shelf sitters. There are also china single children and pairs, children musicians, and dancing girls.

Many Oriental children figurines were also manufactured and also figurines produced to imitate Blue Delft wares.

When buying Occupied Japan pieces, look for the better quality workmanship (some of it is very crude). The bisque pieces tend to be of a higher quality than the china ones. Choose pieces without cracks, repairs, or nicks, and with the paint still intact.

Marks:

Authentic pieces are stamped "Made in Occupied Japan" or "Occupied Japan" under the final clear glaze of china pieces and on the surface of bisque pieces. These marks are known to have been added to pieces that are not genuine. You can test the authenticity of a mark on glazed china pieces by trying to remove the marks with acetone (nail polish remover). This test cannot be done on bisque pieces. More information can be obtained from the Occupied Japan Collectors Club listed at the back of this book.

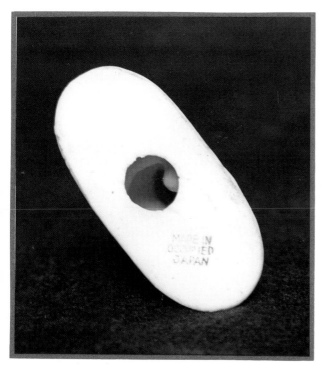

Occupied Japan mark.

Boy and girl china "shelf sitters" sitting on bench, 4" high, marked "Made Occupied Japan" and a manufacturer's mark. *Author's collection. Photo by Diane Freer.*

China boy with dog (3⅞" high) and girl with chicken (3¾" high) pair. Stamped "Made in Occupied Japan" in black on bottom. *Author's collection. Photo by Diane Freer.*

China girl with dog, 2½" high, stamped "Made in Occupied Japan." *Collection of Linda Rehak and Andrew Swanson. Photo by Laurie Morrison.*

Dutch girl, China, 4¾" high, stamped "Made in Occupied Japan" in black ink on bottom. *Author's collection. Photo by Diane Freer.*

Bisque girl figurine attached to vase. Crudely painted. Stamped "Made in Occupied Japan" in black ink on bottom. Approximately 2" high. *Previously part of author's collection. Photo by Diane Freer.*

China girl with purse attached to vase. Some gilt decoration. 2" high, stamped "Made in Occupied Japan." *Collection of Linda Rehak and Andrew Swanson. Photo by Laurie Morrison.*

Hummel-type boy in *lederhosen* going for a hike. China, 4" high, stamped "Made in Occupied Japan." *Collection of Linda Rehak and Andrew Swanson. Photo by Laurie Morrison.*

Boy dressed as a cowboy with a ceramic pot. China, 5¼" high, stamped "Made in Occupied Japan" in red on bottom. *Author's collection. Photo by Diane Freer.*

Chapter 14

All-Bisque Dolls—First Cousin to Bisque Figurines

I would be remiss without mentioning bisque dolls. Clearly, bisque figurines and bisque dolls are first cousins. Many German manufacturers used the same molds for their doll's heads as they did for their figurines. This is easy to see when you compare a Gebruder Heubach piano baby head with some of their doll heads. Kewpies are another example where the close relationship is so evident.

All-bisque Bonnet doll. *Author's collection. Photo by Diane Freer.*

The primary difference between bisque dolls and figurines is one of movement—the dolls have arms or legs that are hinged, their heads might turn, and they may bend at the waist. They often had molded hair and clothes as the figurines did (these are the most desirable, particularly those in white underwear with ruffles) but many were meant to be dressed as other dolls.

All-bisque dolls tend to be small, like most figurines, and date from approximately the same time (1870s-1940s). It would be hard to be a figurine collector and not have at least a passing interest in bisque dolls.

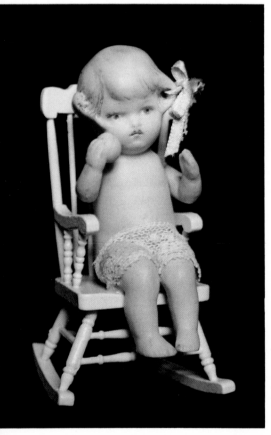

Small bisque doll with molded hair and clothing. *Collection of Rose Marie Willruth. Photo by Laurie Morrison.*

All-Bisque doll with drooping bloomers, German. *Author's collection. Photo by Diane Freer.*

Small bisque doll. *Collection of Linda Rebak and Andrew Swanson. Photo by Laurie Morrison.*

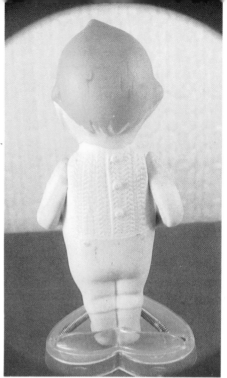

Small all-bisque doll with molded clothing. *Collection of Rose Marie Willruth. Photo by Laurie Morrison.*

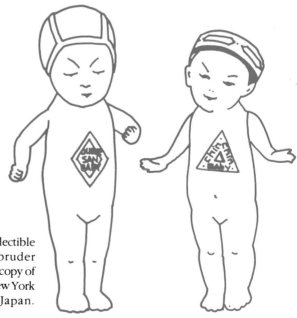

"Chin Chin Baby" is a very collectible bisque doll made by Gebruder Heubach. "Que San Baby" is a copy of that doll by Morimura Bros., New York importers of dolls from Japan. *Illustration by Kathy Fable.*

All-bisque German twins dolls. Both have broken left leg. *Collection of Jenny Jones. Photo by Jim Yarbrough.*

All-bisque black baby dolls. Japanese, circa 1930. *Collection of Jenny Jones. Photo by Jim Yarbrough.*

All-bisque black "tinies." *Collection of Jenny Jones. Photo by Jim Yarbrough.*

Chapter 15

How to Clean Bisque and China Figurines

The best way to keep your figurines clean is to keep them stored in a glass case. This will protect them not only from dirt but from accidental breakage. Dusting them with a good quality artist's or camera brush is also a good idea.

The cleaning of china figurines is easy—they can be wiped with a damp cloth or even with mildly soapy water.

Bisque figurines, however, do pose a problem. As the decoration on bisque was applied after the figurine was fired, any sort of rubbing may disturb it. If possible, it is better not to clean your bisque figurines, but if you must, be very cautious. Try to use a *dry* cloth first to remove dirt and dust. If this doesn't work, use the same method as described above for china, but try it in a very small area first to be certain you won't be doing damage to the decoration or your figurine.

Organizations of Interest

Society of Nativists, Wassail House, 64 Severn Road, Cardiff CF1 9EA, Wales, UK.
International group with an American chapter since 1988. Members collect or make Christmas creche which often includes bisque figurines. Write for information.

Bonniebrook Historical Society, Box 263, Branson, MO 65616
The purpose of the Bonniebrook Historical Society is to rebuild Rose O'Neill's home and to maintain it as a museum.

International Rose O'Neill Club, Box 668, Branson, MO 65616
Membership in the IROC entitles one to the newsletter "Kewpiesta Kourier", 4 times a year. The organization runs a "Kewpiesta" in Branson, MO. every April with attendees from all over the world. The organization also offers an art scholarship to talented students.

Occupied Japan Collector's Club, 29 Freeborn Street, Newport, Rhode Island 02840

Auction House Galleries

The following auction houses have toy and doll auctions or general antique auctions which may include figurines. Write to them for information on how to suscribe to their auction catalogs:

Bonham's, Montpelier Street, London SW7 1HH, England

Richard A. Bourne, Box 141, Hyannisport, MA 02647

Butterfield and Butterfield, 220 San Bruno Blvd, San Francisco, CA 94103

Christie's East, 219 E. 67th Street, New York, NY 10021

Christie's South Kensington, 95 Old Brompton Road, London SW7 3LD, U.K.

Frasher's, Rte. 1, Box 141, Oak Grove, MO 64075

Hart Galleries, 3211 Westheimer, Houston, TX 77098

James D. Julia, Inc., Box 830, Fairfield, ME 04937

Marvin Cohen, Box 425, Rte. 20 and 22, New Lebanon, NY 12125

McMaster's, Box 1775, Cambridge, OH 43725

Skinner Galleries, Rte. 117, Bolton, MA 01740

Sotheby's, 1334 York Avenue, New York, NY 10012

Sotheby's, 34-35 New Bond Street, London W1A 2AA, U.K.

Theriault's, Box 151, Annapolis, MD 21414

Richard W. Withington, RD 2, Box 440, Hillsboro, NH 03244

Glossary of Terms

Bisque—(the correct name is really biscuit ware)—is unglazed porcelain that has been fired only once. Bisque has a dull finish and can be decorated with various colors.

China—is the commonly used term for glazed porcelain. It originally referred to porcelain wares from China.

Déposé or *Dep*—means this design is a copyrighted trademark. It was used in France, Germany, and Austria.

Intaglio eyes—incised eyes that are painted to have a realistic look.

Marks—any number, manufacturer's name, initials, symbol, or country of origin mark that appears on a figurine.

Molded clothing—clothing on a figurine that is sculptured into the original mold.

Molded hair—hair on a figurine that was sculptured into the original mold.

Mohair wig—while most German figurines had molded hair, some were designed to wear wigs made of mohair.

Porcelain—hard-fired ceramic ware that is translucent when held up to the light. Made with an important ingredient called Kaolin.

Tinted bisque—Bisque that has a colorant added to it to give it a rosy color.

Bibliography

Books

Angione, Genevieve, *All Bisque and Half-Bisque Dolls,* 5th Edition, Exton: Schiffer Publishing, 1981.

Axe, John, *Kewpies—Dolls and Art,* Cumberland: Hobby House Press, 1978.

Borger, Mona, *China—Dolls for Study and Admiration,* San Francisco: Borger Publications, 1983

Cieslik, Jurgen and Marianne, *German Doll Encyclopedia 1800-1939,* Cumberland: Hobby House Press, 1985.

Cieslik, Jurgen and Marianne, *German Doll Marks and Identification Book,* Cumberland: Hobby House Press, 1986.

Collier, Judy and Martie Cook, *Official Identifier and Price Guide to Antique and Modern Dolls,* 4th Edition. New York: House of Collectibles, 1989.

Early, Ray and Eilene, *Snow Babies,* Westerville: Ray and Eilene Early, 1983.

Florence, Gene, *The Collector's Encyclopedia of Occupied Japan Collectibles,* Paducah, Kentucky: Collectors Books, 1976.

Foulke, Jan, *8th Blue Book Dolls & Values,* Cumberland: Hobby House Press, 1987.

Foulke, Jan, *Focusing on Dolls,* Cumberland: Hobby House Press, 1988.

Heininger, Mary Lynn Stevens and others, *A Century of Childhood 1820-1920,* Rochester: Strong Museum, 1984.

Heyerdahl, Virigina Ann, editor, *The Best of Doll Reader,* Cumberland: Hobby House Press, 1982.

Heyerdahl, Virginia Ann, editor, *The Best of Doll Reader, Part II,* Cumberland: Hobby House Press, 1986.

Heyerdahl, Virginia Ann, editor, *The Best of Doll Reader, Part III,* Cumberland: Hobby House Press, 1988.

Hudgeons, Thomas A. (III), editor, *Official Price Guide to Pottery,* Orlando: House of Collectibles, 1985.

Husfloen, Kyle, editor, *Antique Trader Antiques and Collectibles Price Guide,* Dubuque, Iowa: Babka Publishing, 1989.

Huxford, Sharon and Bob, editors, *Schroeder's Antique Price Guide,* Paducah, Kentucky: Collector Books, 1990.

Kovel, Ralph and Terry, *Kovel's Dictionary of Marks*, New York: Crown Publishers, 1986.

Kovel, Ralph and Terry, *Kovel's Antiques and Collectibles Price List*, New York: Crown Publishers, 1990.

Kovel, Ralph and Terry, *Kovel's Collectors' Source Book*, New York: Crown Publishers, 1983.

Johl, Janet Pagter, *Still More About Dolls*, New York: H. L. Lindquist Publications, 1950.

Lavitt, Wendy, *The Knopf Collector's Guides to American Antiques/Dolls*, New York: Alfred A. Knopf, Inc., 1983.

Longest, David, *Character Toys & Collectibles*, Paducah, Kentucky: Collectors Books, 1984.

MacFarland, Grace, *Official Price Guide to Antiques and Other Collectibles*, Orlando: House of Collectibles, 1981.

Miller, Robert, *Wallace-Homestead 1986/87 Price Guide to Dolls*, Lombard: Wallace-Homestead Book Company, 1986.

Savage, George and Harold Newman, John Cushion, *An Illustrated Dictionary of Ceramics*, London: Thames and Hudson, 1985.

Smith, Partrica, *German Dolls Identification and Values*, Paducah, Kentucky: Collector's Books, 1985.

Smith, Patricia, *Doll Values Antique to Modern*, Paducah, Kentucky: Collector's Books, 1990.

Stanton, Carol Ann, *Heubach's Little Characters*, Middlesex, England: Living Doll's Publications Ltd., 1978.

St. George, Eleanor, *The Dolls of Yesterday*, New York: Charles Scribner's Sons, 1948.

Theriault, Florence, *Parlour Fancies*, Annapolis: Theriault's, 1990.

Werner, Norma and Freida Marion, *The Collector's Encyclopedia of Half-Dolls*, Crown Publishers, New York: 1979.

Articles

Crowley, Jean H. "Snow Babies," *Spinning Wheel*, January-February, 1970.

Crowley, Jean H. "Continuing Research of the Snow Babies," *Spinning Wheel*, 1970.

Crowley, Jean H. "More About Snow Babies," *Spinning Wheel*, December 1971.

Jacoby, Daniel, "B. Shackman and Company: Snowbabies and Related Figurines," *Antique Trader Weekly*, January 28, 1987.

Index

Price Guide

This guide is provided to give you some idea of the prices you might expect to pay for figurines in this book. Market prices may vary in different parts of the country, due to the economy and other factors. Please use this as a tool to help you decide what to pay but not as a firm price list.

GENERAL FIGURINES

Pg. 8	Limbach boy	$150-185
	Boy with soccer ball	$50-95
Pg. 9	Girl with blue gown	$250-325
	School girl	$85-150
Pg. 10	Bisque sweeper	$100-175
Pg. 11	Girl in lace dress	$50-110
Pg. 13	Boy in egg	$200-300
Pg. 14	Boy with school book	$75-110
Pg. 15	Pair of children	$90-150
	Girl with basket	$75-135
	Morning stretch	$45-85
Pg. 16	Baby in basket	$350-500
	Black boy	$300-400
Pg. 17	Dutch girl	$45-100
	Boy in bathtub	$35-85
Pg. 18	Babies in carriages	$250-350
	Girl on horn	$75-120
Pg. 19	Boy in suitcase	$85-135
	Boys in bathtub	$45-95 each
Pg. 20	Bisque girls on chamber pots	$100-160 each
	Black baby in blanket	$90-140
Pg. 21	Figurine on potty	$135-195
	Boy with chamber pot	$100-165
Pg. 22	China angels	$35-95 each
	Children with umbrellas	$250-325
	Cherub	$35-95

PIANO BABIES

Pg. 23	Parian piano baby	$60-125
Pg. 24	Piano baby with dog	$65-100
Pg. 25	Piano baby sucking thumb	$65-100
Pg. 26	"Papa's darling"	$75-125
Pg. 27	German piano baby with dog and rattle	$65-100
	Japanese piano baby	$35-75
	Piano baby with dog	$95-135
Pg. 28	Girl with apple	$110-175
	Boy with rattle	$85-135
Pg. 29	Boy with legs in air	$85-110
Pg. 30	Piano baby with bib	$65-110
	Piano baby with grapes	$200-300
Pg. 31	Large piano baby	$225-230
Pg. 32	Black piano baby	$95-145
	Crawling piano baby	$175-225
Pg. 33	Large seated girls	$175-225
	Large girl with cup	$200-300
Pg. 34	Two piano babies	$75-135 each
	Piano baby with Siamese kittens	$175-225
	Baby in walker	$95-145
Pg. 35	Pair of piano babies lying down	$150-200 each
	Pair of Japanese piano babies	$55-95 pair
Pg. 36	Piano baby with wig	$110-185
	Parian type baby	$65-95
Pg. 37	Pair of Japanese babies	$50-95 pair
	Baby in crib	$65-95
Pg. 38	Parian piano baby	$65-110
	Piano baby girl with dog	$150-20-0

HEUBACH FIGURINES

Pg. 40	Baby with shower cap	$225-300
Pg. 41	Baby in tub	$150-200

Pg. 42	Hugging position babies	$200-300
	Pointing position babies	$200-300
Pg. 43	Seated Dutch girl	$150-200
	Easter Bunny children	$300-700 each
	Baby in shoe	$250-500
Pg. 44	Girl with dog	$700-900
	Girl and boy pair	$800-1200
Pg. 46	Girl and boy busts	$600-900
Pg. 47	Two snow babies	$125-175 each
	Dutch boy	$100-200
Pg. 48	Dancing girl	$250-350
Pg. 49	Pair of black boys	$800-1000
Pg. 50	Baby Stuart	$145-200
	Two seated piano babies	lg. $225-300
		sm. $125-200
Pg. 51	Large girl figurine	$900-1200
	Boy figurines	$800-1100
Pg. 54	Black boy with corn	$500-700

TRINKET BOXES/FAIRING PIECES

Pg. 53	Heubach powder box	$200-250
Pg. 54	Trinket box	$125-195
Pg. 55	"tug of war"	$135-210
	Kewpie trinket box	$185-275
Pg. 56	German trinket box	$185-210
	U.S. Pottery box no price available	
Pg. 57	Child on bureau	$195-275

FIGURINES WITH RECEPTACLES

Pg. 58	Boy with hat in hand	$85-135
Pg. 59	Two bisque boys	blue $65-110,
		pink $85-135
	Half-figurine planter	$35-65
Pg. 60	Girl with baskets	$65-110
	Boy with boot	$45-85
Pg. 61	Two girls with receptacles	$65-95 each
	Figurine with vase	$85-115
Pg. 62	Boy holding planter	$35-65
	Girl with cast	$65-95
Pg. 63	Musical pair	$35-55
	Boy and girl planter	$45-75

FIGURINES FROM CHILDREN'S BOOK ILLUSTRATIONS

Pg. 64	Mother Goose figurines	$45-95 each
Pg. 65	Boy writing on slate	$45-95
	Two figurines in nightclothes	$35-85
	Girl with arms around legs	$35-85
Pg. 66	Boy leaning on elbow	$50-95
Pg. 67	Boy in top hat	$35-85
	Lying girl in nightclothes	$35-85
	Kneeling girl in nightclothes	$35-85
	Girl in bonnet	$35-85

SUNBONNET BABIES

Pg. 68	Girl doing wash	$175-300
Pg. 70	Girl with rug beater	$175-300

KEWPIES

Pg. 74	Kewpie in inkwell	$500-700
	Kewpie in hammock	$250-325

Pg. 75	Kewpie in box	$500-700
Pg.77	The Thinker	$300-400
	Kewpie with guitar	$225-300
Pg. 78	Kewpies with insects	$300-400 each
	Kneeling Kewpie	$225-300
	Kewpie with book	$300-400
Pg. 79	Kewpie tea party	$325-500
	Kewpie with cat	$325-400
	Lying down Kewpie	$250-325
Pg. 80	Hottentot doll	$500-600
	Japanese doll	$30-75
	Kewpie policeman	$350-450
Pg. 81	Kewpie perfume bottles	$400-500 each
	Kewpie in chair with Doodle dog	$800-1200
	Kewpie in chair	$300-400
Pg. 82	Tiny Kewpie	$75-150
	Kewpie on swan	$325-450
Pg. 83	Kewpie with candy container	$250-350
	Kewpie dolls	$225-350 each
Pg. 84	Trinket box	$250-350
	The Traveller	$300-400
	Leaping Kewpie	$250-300
	Miniature Kewpies	$250-300 each
Pg. 85	Kewpie aviator	$275-300
	Bride and groom	$300-425
	Kewpie on bench	$350-475
	Kewpie on chair	$175-400
Pg. 86	Three Japanese "Kewpies"	$25-50 each
	Japanese, one with bottle	$25-50 each
Pg. 87	4 Japanese "Kewpies"	$325-65 each
	Japanese huggers	$50-75
	Kewpie soldier	$475-600
Pg. 88	Two Sweepers	sm. $275-350
		lg. $325-400
	Kewpie with Doodle dog	$800-1200
	Japanese "Kewpie"	$50-75
Pg. 89	Kewpie with basket	$250-375
	Kewpie with book	$275-400
	Kewpie-related no price available	
	Kewpie in hair with mandolin	$325-420
	Blunderbloo on sled	$325-400

SNOW BABIES

Pg. 91	Crawling snow baby	$95-125
	Baby with sled	$85-135
Pg. 92	Seated baby	$140-175
p.g 94	Two babies on sled	$175-225
Pg. 95	Group of tiny snow babies	$50-100 each
	Snow babies on sled	$85-135 each
Pg. 100	Cliquot Club	$250-300
Pg. 101	Japanese babies	$45-85 each
	No-snow on sleds	$85-120 each
Pg. 102	2 babies on sled	$125-200
	Large and small baby on sled	$125-200
	Girl and boy on sleds	$100-175 each
Pg. 103	Two babies on two sleds	lg. $85-12
		sm. $75-100
	Two babies on one sled	$90-145
	One seated, one lying down on sled	$100-160
Pg. 104	No snows with bears	$100-175 each
	Japanese babies with bears	$60-85 set
Pg. 105	Baby on bear	$150-225
	and small bear	$35-50
	Three babies on bear	$75-145
	Baby with two bears	$35-85 each
Pg. 107	Snow baby candle holder	$50-75
	Snow baby dolls	$175-275 feach
Pg. 109	Baby with seal, German	$50-110
	Baby with seal, Japanese	$25-50
	Baby with penguins	$125-175
	Baby with reindeer babies	$200-275
Pg. 110	Dancing babies	$100-175
	Three standing babies	$85-145 each
Pg. 111	Two standing babies	$110-175 each
	Snow baby globes	$30-100 each
Pg. 112	Repro snow baby twins	$15-35
	Snow baby twins	$85-120
	Snow suit twins	$35-65
Pg. 113	Carollers	$90-150
	Children with bell	$85-135
	Santa with child	$85-135
Pg. 114	Santa and sled	$90-135
	Igloo	$95-145
	Babies on hill	$120-165
	Santa with two children	$110-165

	Baby pyramid	$100-155
Pg. 115	Snow boy skier	$110-185
	Christmas tree ornament	$30-60
	No-snow skater	$50-100
	Two figures on sled	$65-100
	One child on sled	$60-95
Pg. 116	Rubber Molded	No price available
Pg. 117	Penguins	$45-65
	No-snows on wall	$125-160
	Black snow baby	$100-200
	Seated baby	$85-135
Pg. 118	Three seated babies	$95-125
	Two surprised babies	$75-110
	Seated snow baby	$45-80
Pg. 119	Girl and boy seated	$100-175 each
	Four little babies	$65-95 each
	Leaning babies	lg. $90-125
		sm. $45-90
Pg. 120	Boxed set	$30-50
	Two babies with snow balls	$90-145 each
Pg. 121	Lying hooded baby	$95-145
	Hooded baby with stroller	$110-170
	Two reproduction babies	$15-25 each
Pg. 122	Two repro babies (top of Pg.)	$15-25 each
	Two repro babies (bottom of Pg.)	$20-40each
Pg. 123	Three Japanese snow babies	$30-55 each
	Jointed snow baby	$225-300

FROZEN CHARLOTTES

Pg. 125	Group of small Charlottes	$25-60 each
Pg. 126	Large frozen Charley	$600-900
Pg. 127	Black frozen Charley	$90-125
Pg. 128	China Charlotte	$70-100
Pg. 130	Two Charlottes	$30-70 each
Pg. 131	Stone bisque Charley	$40-65
Pg. 133	Charley with shorts	$300-400
Pg. 134	Three Charlottes in dresses	lg. $200-325
		sm. $85-125 each
	Four tiny Charlottes	$35-85 (all four)
Pg. 135	"Old woman in Shoe"	No price available
	Collection in box	$250-450
Pg. 136	Large Charley	$300-450
Pg. 137	Collection in box	$300-500
	Group of Charlottes	$40-150 each
Pg. 140	Oriental Charley	$300-500

IMMOBILES AND CHARACTER FIGURINES

Pg. 141	Flapper girl	$20-40
	Oriental girl	$25-45
Pg. 142	Flapper girl	$20-40
	Boy in red pants	$25-45
Pg. 143	Boy with goggles	$25-45
	Cowboy and girl	$15-35 each

NODDERS AND SWAYERS

Pg. 144	Girl swayer	$150-225
Pg. 145	Girl with dolls	$175-225
	Baby in bunting	$250-400
Pg. 146	Three comic figures	$85-125 each
	Lady with purse	$35-75
Pg. 147	Two comic figures	$85-125 each
Pg. 148	Nodder family	$450-800

HALF DOLLS

Pg. 149	Young girl	$40-85
Pg. 150	Girl with doll	$90-125
Pg. 151	Girl with flower	$50-75
Pg. 153	Girl with banana curls	$65-85
	Girl with posies	$65-85
	Gretel	$60-85
Pg. 154	School boy	$100-175

NAUGHTY FIGURINES

Pg. 155-57		$85-150 each

OCCUPIED JAPAN

Pg. 158	Girl with staff	$15-30
Pg. 160	Boy and girl on bench	$30-50
	Boy and girl set	$30-50 (for pair)
Pg. 161	Girl with dog	$12-22
	Dutch girl	$15-30
	Girl with vase	$10-30
Pg. 162	Girl with vase	$10-25
	Hummel-type boy	$20-40
	Cowboy	$20-30